D0606055

the button *maker*

the button *maker*

**30 great techniques and
35 stylish projects**

Sarah Beaman

COLLINS & BROWN

First published in Great Britain in 2006 by
Collins & Brown Ltd
151 Freston Road
London
W10 6TH

An imprint of Anova Books Company Ltd

Distributed in the United States and Canada by Sterling Publishing Co,
387 Park Avenue South,
New York, NY 10016 USA

1 3 5 7 9 8 6 4 2

British Library Cataloguing-in-Publication Data: A catalogue record for
this book is available from the British Library

ISBN-13: 9 781843 402770
ISBN-10: 1 84340 277 7

EDITOR: Fiona Corbridge
DESIGNER: Lotte Oldfield
STYLE PHOTOGRAPHY: Lucinda Symons
STEPS PHOTOGRAPHY: Matthew Dickens

Reproduction by Classicscan Pte Ltd
Printed and bound in China by SNP Leefung

contents

introduction

This book demonstrates how to make lovely buttons – from many different materials and employing a wide variety of techniques – for all sorts of projects. Whatever your level of skill, there is something here for you.

Your own buttons can add real individuality and personality to a project. They are a way of expressing something about yourself in a relatively unassuming manner – you can use them to make a statement without going over the top. For the person who sews, making a button can become an extension of a sewing project, utilizing much of the same material and equipment. But even if you are a non-sewer, the small scale of button-making projects makes them easy to approach. It is not necessary to have lots of specialist tools, just enthusiasm and creativity. Remember to think small. Choose fine threads and closely woven fabrics in proportion to the scale of the button, or the results may look clumsy.

Each chapter in this book deals with buttons in a different type of material. It starts with a techniques section containing photographic step-by-step guidelines for making buttons, and then features projects that you can make yourself. Most of the materials are available from haberdasheries and craft shops; a resource list at the back of the book will help you track down mail-order suppliers.

Whether simple or complex, much pleasure is to be gained from making and using handmade buttons. I hope this book will provide the inspiration for you to make buttons to adorn all kinds of projects, adapting and elaborating on the ideas to reflect your own taste. A handmade button is a sure-fire way of turning a ready-made item into something special, or can provide the finishing touch for a lovingly made piece of work.

Happy button-making!

Sarah Beaman

customizing existing buttons

This is a quick and easy way to turn a very ordinary button into something special, personalizing it to give it a whole new life. Buttons can be embellished in many ways, so unleash your creativity and have fun!

photographs and transfers

Flat buttons with a shank become miniature photo frames when an image is glued on: great for use in card-making, scrapbooks or heirloom projects. Use photocopies of precious photographs rather than originals. Cut them out neatly or use a craft punch for a really accurate circle. Rub-down transfers are enjoying a big revival and can easily be applied to smooth buttons.

painting, gilding and burning

Painting is perhaps one of the most obvious ways to add interest to a button. You can paint in the existing design or add your own motif to a plain button. Use enamel paint if the button needs to be washable. Try gilding buttons for a glamorous metallic finish, or use a pyrography tool on wooden buttons for a more rustic result.

gems

Flat-backed paste gems are readily available in a variety of shapes and colours, and instantly make dull buttons look wonderful. Use superglue to attach them and make your own expensive-looking jewelled buttons.

fabric covers

These plastic buttons consist of two separate components. Cover the centre in fabric to coordinate with your project and then simply snap the parts back together. Look through the family button box and you may find some vintage examples that are just right for a re-vamp.

stickers and charms

There are endless stickers available, which can be applied to make great decorative buttons, and no glue is required! It is also possible to find flat metal charms, such as this Celtic motif (below left), which can be stuck on with superglue.

natural objects

Some natural objects lend themselves to becoming buttons, often with minimal work, so keep your eyes open. Here dried yellow beans and betel nuts (below), both from an Asian supermarket, have been drilled to make holes for stitching through. Small pieces of slate, acorn cups and a variety of dried pips and seeds might also make good candidates.

applying new covers

Transform dreary buttons by covering them with inexpensive badges. The pins from the backs of the badges are easily removed with pliers, and superglue will hold the new coverings in place.

Plain buttons with a shank will serve as a device to carry flat items. Old coins are often very decorative: use superglue to stick them to plain buttons.

Make a button that can be used as a seal. This one (above left) is made from a melted coloured hot-glue stick and will remain flexible, unlike traditional sealing wax. Make the seal on baking parchment; peel it off when cool then glue in place.

making buttons

Although customizing buttons is a good way of personalizing them, it's fun to create your own and they will add a really special, unique touch to a project. Use your imagination to create buttons that will be a real focal point.

A selection of handmade buttons.

button-formers

Many buttons require some sort of mould or former to support the work. A wide variety of materials can be used for this purpose, sometimes remaining visible when the button is completed, but more often being concealed with a decorative covering. The finished button must be firm so that it will not slip back through the buttonhole when it is fastened. Some materials are shown on the right, but you can experiment with other materials such as washers, slices of cork (sand to shape), old buttons and wooden rawlplugs.

making a solid back

All buttons need to be constructed so that they can be sewn on to a garment or project. The formers used to make some types of handmade button mean that a hollow will be left at the back of the button, making this impossible. To overcome this, make a solid back following the technique illustrated in Making a Solid Back with a Woven Shank (see page 87).

- *Mount board squares*
- *Wooden beads*
- *Stuffed-ball mould*
- *Purchased wooden heart*
- *Hand-cut wood blanks and dowel*
- *Metal and plastic rings*
- *A selection of metal and plastic self-cover moulds*
- *Plastic loom-type mould*
- *Rimmed button moulds*

Using a self-cover button mould

This is one of the easiest ways of creating a button. Self-cover button moulds, or button-formers, are made from metal or plastic in a range of sizes. Cover them in self-fabric (the same fabric used on the garment or project) for an understated fastening, or use them as a foundation for more decorative techniques. This type of mould is not suitable for very thick or stiff fabrics.

Covering the front of the button mould

If your fabric is semi-transparent, it will be necessary to line the button mould to ensure that it will be concealed. Fine fabrics also benefit from a lining layer. It is usually possible to hold the two layers of fabric together and work the gathering thread through them simultaneously.

1. Cut out the template from the pack (choose the appropriate size). Place it on the fabric and draw around it with a fabric-marking pencil. If using patterned fabric, check that the design or motif is centred.

2. Thread a needle with strong thread and work a running stitch a little way in from the edge of the circle. Pull the ends of the thread to gather up the edge a little.

3. Place the button face down in the centre of the fabric circle. Pull the threads tight so that the fabric gathers snugly around the button. (The fabric should be taut around the mould; the back of the button will conceal all the gathers.) Tie the ends of the thread together tightly and trim them close. Check that the button is centred within the fabric covering.

Covering the back of the button mould

The back of the button can also be covered with fabric if you wish, to give a finished look. Use lining fabric if self-fabric is too thick or too thin.

1. Cut out a circle of fabric a little less than twice the diameter of the button back. Fold the circle into quarters and snip a tiny section off the pointed end of the folded fabric. The button shank should just fit through the hole you have cut.

2. Carefully apply a little anti-fray liquid around the edge of the hole. Work a running stitch around the outer edge of the circle as in step 2 (opposite).

3. Place the button back in the centre of the circle and pull the ends of the thread to gather the fabric on the inside of the mould. Check that the two holes are aligned, and then tie off the ends of the thread securely.

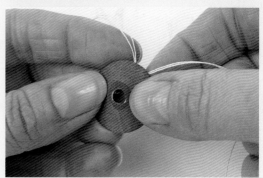

4. To complete the button, assemble the two components by aligning the shank on the button front with the hole on the button back and pushing them together firmly. The back will click into place.

using buttons

Buttons can be used as ornamental, non-functioning features, appearing purely as embellishments on everything from clothing and accessories to jewellery, greetings cards, scrapbooks and papercrafts. They can add a touch of whimsy, naive charm, or an elegant sophisticated edge to a project, depending on the type and style of button selected, and the method of application.

Practicalities

Some of the buttons in this book will endure the rigours of laundering without needing special treatment. Others are not washable, or will not withstand repeated laundering at high temperatures. If you wish to use these buttons on items that are frequently cleaned, they will need to be removed from the item each time. (However, there are ways of making the removal process easier – see below.) If you want to avoid the inconvenience of button removal, use buttons on items that are cleaned infrequently, such as coats and evening wear, and household textiles such as bedspreads and cushions.

Removing buttons for cleaning

Technique 1

Apply a small, flat secondary button to the back of the handmade button (with a thread shank added in between if the handmade button doesn't already have one). Make a buttonhole in the garment, the size of the secondary button. Now the button can be simply unbuttoned to remove it.

If the button is to be used as a closure device,

two overlapping buttonholes are required, one on the buttonhole side (to fit the handmade button) and a small one on the button side (to fit the secondary button). To fasten the item, button the secondary button through the small hole and the handmade button through the regular buttonhole.

Technique 2

Stitch the handmade buttons to a length of ribbon or tape, spacing them as desired, then make buttonholes to fit on both sides of the garment. Position the strip under both layers of the garment and button through the matching sets of buttonholes.

Making sewing holes in a handmade button

Form the holes in the desired position on the first button, and use this as a template for positioning the holes on subsequent buttons. This type of button can be attached in the conventional way, but for a change it can be nice to use a thicker thread (or even ribbon) and knot this on the top of the button to provide extra decorative detail.

Above: Handmade buttons make pretty and unique embellishments for cards, invitations and other papercrafts. They can be sewn, tied or glued in place and bring an interesting three-dimensional quality to the work.

Centre: These nostalgic buttons are an interesting and unusual way to display family portraits in a scrapbook or family heritage project. Tie descriptive tags around them, or button them on to scraps of special fabric or cloth storage pockets containing mementoes.

Below: Handmade buttons make a special gift: present them carefully and they are sure to be well received. Make a set to commemorate a special event such as the birth of a baby or a wedding, and they are bound to become a treasured keepsake.

techniques
and projects

knitted buttons

Knitting yarn is available in a myriad of colours, plies and textures, so the possibilities for buttons are very exciting. A button can be formed out of knitted yarn itself or, alternatively, a piece of knitting can be used to cover a button-former.

Finishing a knitted bobble button

When you knit a bobble to make a button, leave long ends when you cast off: these can be used to sew the button on to the project. If the yarn is fluffy, use small scissors to carefully trim away fibres so that the yarn is smooth.

useful tips

• Whether you choose to use the yarns specified or replace them with an alternative, it is always best to knit a swatch to test the scale. Use the swatch to experiment with swiss darning, also known as duplicate stitch.

• Duplicate stitch must cover the stitch it is being made over, so the yarns must be of a comparative weight. If you wish to use a finer yarn or an embroidery thread, you can double or even triple it to even up the weight.

• Where the yarn is suitable for washing, only gentle hand-washing is recommended. Use your swatch to test for both shrinkage and colour fastness.

symbols and abbreviations

[ ]	Work the stitch(es) in the square brackets the number of times stated.
K2tog	Knit two stitches together.
P2tog	Purl two stitches together.

Creating a motif using the Swiss darning technique

This is a quick and easy way to make a piece of plain stocking stitch knitting look as though it has a pattern or motif knitted into it. Swiss darning is an embroidery stitch that duplicates the pattern of the knit, so the motif appears to be knitted in.

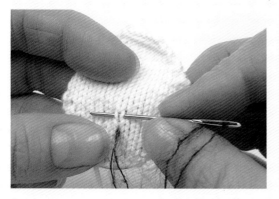

1. Thread a knitter's sewing needle with yarn (here the fine yarn is used double). From back to front, bring the yarn through at the base of the first stitch to be embroidered, leaving a 10cm (4in) tail of yarn at the back. Take the needle around the top of the stitch, going under the base of the stitch above.

2. Take the needle back down through the base of the first stitch to cover it with the yarn.

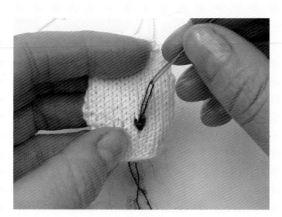

3. Bring the needle out through the base of the stitch above and repeat these steps until the whole vertical row has been embroidered. At the back of the work, weave the yarn through the backs of the embroidery stitches to emerge in position to start the next row.

knitted bobble

Depending upon the type of yarn that is used to create a knitted bobble, you can achieve a variety of different looks. They can be quite small if fine, flat wool is used, or have a textural appearance (as here) because of long fibres that project from the yarn.

Materials

Yarn: Patons Whisper, white

Tools

Knitting needles: 4mm (UK size 8, US size 6)

Scissors

Make a slip knot, leaving a long tail. Knit four times into the front and back of the slip knot (4 stitches).
Row 1: Increase into every stitch (8 stitches).
Starting with a knit row, work 4 rows in stocking stitch.
Row 6: [K2tog], repeat to end of row (4 stitches).
Row 7: Slip 2 stitches purlwise, p2tog, pass slipped stitches over.
Cast off last stitch leaving a long tail.

Tie the long tails together in a firm double knot. Trim the fibres off the tails. Attach the bobble using the tails. (See also Finishing a Knitted Bobble Button, *page 16*.)

OPPOSITE: *These tactile bobble buttons add the finishing touch to a pretty embroidered cardigan. The sheen on the long white fibres of the yarn effectively picks up that of the decorative white beads and sequins.*

heart motif button

This sweet heart motif has been embroidered on a piece of stocking stitch knitting using Swiss darning. This technique, sometimes known as duplicate stitch, replicates the pattern of the knitting.

Materials

Yarn: Rowan Cotton Glace, white; Rowan Kidsilk Haze, dark pink

Self-cover button: 29mm (1⅛in), white plastic

Tools

Knitting needles: 2.75mm, UK size 12 (US size 2)

Scissors

Knitter's sewing needle

to make the background

Knit very firmly throughout.

Using white, cast on 7 stitches by the thumb method.
Row 1: Purl. **Row 2:** Increase into the first stitch, knit to the last stitch, increase into the last stitch (9 stitches). Repeat rows 1–2 four times, then repeat row 1 once more (17 stitches). **Row 12:** Knit. **Row 13:** Purl.
Row 14: K2tog, knit to the last two stitches, k2tog. Repeat rows 13–14 four times, then repeat row 13 once more (7 stitches). Cast off.

to embroider the heart motif

Using dark pink, doubled, follow the chart and embroider the heart motif on the white background. The fine yarn is used double to ensure that the embroidery stitch covers the knitted stitch. Embroider the central vertical row first, then the rows on either side. (See Creating a Motif using the Swiss Darning Technique, *page 17.*)

Cover the button blank with the embroidered knitting in the usual way, making sure that the motif remains in shape and centred on the button face. (See Using a Self-Cover Button Mould, *page 10.*)

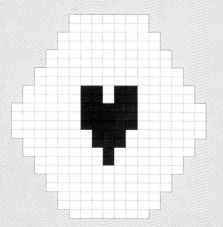

OPPOSITE: *You can use this technique to make a button that exactly matches a piece of knitting. Here, the heart button has been created in different yarns to those of the background, adding extra interest and giving the motif a tactile quality.*
It is easy to make a variety of simple motifs: copy the chart and use it to plot motifs such as spirals, diamonds, noughts and crosses, and flowers.

crocheted buttons

Crocheted buttons have been in and out of fashion for many years. Motifs are worked like a miniature doily, and as they can be relatively thick, are usually mounted over a mould. The size of the crochet hook, thickness of the thread, and size of the mould affect the size of the finished button. For best results, keep the tension firm.

useful tips

- Before you start a crochet button project, or if you wish to use an alternative yarn, crochet a test button to check the pattern for tension and scale. The patterns are easily adapted for different threads, hook sizes or individual tension. If the test button doesn't make up exactly the right size try using a different mould size, thread size or hook, or add or delete a round or two of crochet.
- The nature of the crochet means that the button mould may be visible through the finished covering, so ensure that the mould is attractive in its own right, or is covered in a suitable fabric. You could use a stuffed ball mould for the pearl button, see page 9.
- In the case of an Irish Rose button the covering is too thick to be caught into the back of a commercial mould, so it forms a cap over the whole mould. It is held in place with two rounds of decrease which causes the crochet to collapse towards the centre back of the mould, thereby holding the mould in place.

abbreviations & symbols

[ ]	Work the stitch(es) in the square brackets the number of times stated.
* *	Marks the beginning and end of a sequence. Repeat the sequence between the asterisks as many times as necessary to reach the end of the row.
dc	Double crochet (US single crochet)
sl st	Slip stitch
ch	Chain
sk	Skip
tr	Treble crochet (US double crochet)
lp	Loop
htr	Half treble crochet (US half double crochet)

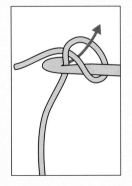 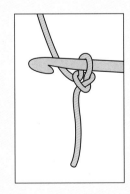

Start off by making a slipknot: make a loop near the end of the yarn; then insert the hook into the loop from front to back and draw another loop through it (above left). Pull the knot close to the hook, but not too tight (above right).

Chain (ch)

To make a chain (ch), wrap the yarn round the hook from back to front (this is called yarn round hook, or yrh) and draw it through the loop on the hook (above). This makes one chain stitch.

Slip stitch (sl st)

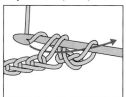

Insert the hook into a stitch or chain (always remember to insert the hook under both strands of the stitch), yarn round hook from the back to the front of the hook, now draw the hook through the stitch and the loop on the hook. You are left with just one loop on the hook. This is one slip stitch.

Double crochet (dc)

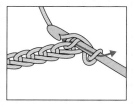 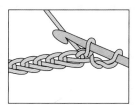

Insert the hook into the second chain from the hook, yarn round hook, draw the loop through your work (above left), yarn round hook and draw the hook through both loops on the hook (above right). You are left with one loop on the hook. This is one double crochet. Repeat into the next stitch or chain. Work until the very last chain. This is one row of double crochet. At the end of the row, make one chain stitch – this is your turning chain – turn the work and work one dc into each stitch of the previous row, ensuring you insert the hook under both loops of the stitch you are crocheting into.

Half treble (htr)

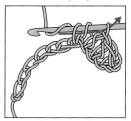

Yarn round hook before inserting the hook into the third chain from the hook, yarn round hook, draw one loop through the work, yarn round hook, draw through all three loops on the hook, leaving just one loop on the hook. This is one half treble.

Making a ring

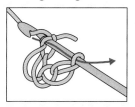

To make a ring, make a series of chains and join the last chain to the first with a slip stitch (above left).

Treble (tr)

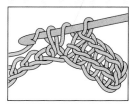 

This stitch is taller yet. As with the half treble, start by wrapping the yarn around the hook and insert the hook into the fourth chain from the hook, yarn round hook, draw one loop through the work (above left), yarn round hook, draw through the first two loops on the hook, yarn round hook, draw through the remaining two loops on the hook (above right), leaving just one loop on the hook. This is one treble. When you reach the end of the row, make three chains. These count as the first stitch of the next row. Turn the work and miss the first treble of the previous row; insert the hook into the second stitch of the new row. Continue to work until the end of the row, inserting the last treble into the top of the turning chain of the row below.

pearl button

In the 1900s these buttons were favoured by Parisian prostitutes, who hung them from their clothing so that the movement attracted attention as they walked! Wherever they are used, the beauty of these buttons still draws our eyes to them. Small pearl beads, which are just visible through the crochet, are used as the moulds.

Materials

Rayon stranded embroidery thread: cream

White glass pearl beads: 8mm (⁵⁄₁₆in), quantity as required

Tools

Crochet hook: 1.00mm UK size 5½/6 (US size 11/12 steel)

Using a single strand of thread:

Rnd 1: In loop start, make 5 dc. Sl st to join. Pull tail to tighten centre.

Rnd 2: Ch 2 (counts as first dc). * 2 dc in each dc * around. Do not join (10 stitches).

Rnds 3, 4, 5: * 1 dc in first and second dc, 2 dc in third dc * around. Weave beginning of tail into inside of work (13, 17, 22 stitches).

Rnds 6, 7, 8, 9: * Dc * around (22 stitches each).

Rnd 10: * Dc in first and second dc, sk next dc * around. Insert the pearl mould.

Rnd 11: * Dc in first and second dc, sk next dc * until all stitches are used.

Shank: Ch 3, sl st in first ch. Fasten off.

OPPOSITE: *These pearl buttons look especially pretty on a wedding or christening gown. Satin or matt embroidery thread comes in a wonderful array of shades; here a lustrous variety was used.*

irish rose button

The Irish rose design was popular in Edwardian times, when it was common to make buttons at home by following patterns printed in contemporary women's magazines. Multiple layers of crochet create the petal effect; a loop is formed behind one petal, over which the petal of the next round is formed. The mould is a button covered in contrasting cotton fabric.

Materials

Crochet cotton: no. 20, in light blue

Self-cover buttons: 29mm (1⅛in), covered in navy blue chambray cotton, quantity as desired

Tools

Crochet hook: 1.00mm UK size 5½/6 (US size 11/12 steel)

Rnd 1: Ch 8, sl st to form ring.

Rnd 2: Ch 5. [Tr, ch 2] seven times in ring. Sl st in third ch of ch 5 to join (8 loops).

Rnd 3: Ch 1 (counts as first dc). * [dc, 5 tr, dc] over ch 2 * around.

Rnd 4: Without turning work, * working behind petals ch 3, sl st between 2 petals * around. (8 loops).

Rnd 5: Sl st into lp. Ch 1 (counts as first dc). * [Dc, 7 tr, dc] over ch 3 lp * around.

Rnd 6: * Working behind petals ch 4, sl st between 2 petals * around (8 loops).

Rnd 7: Sl st into lp. Ch 1 (counts as first dc). * [Dc, htr, 9 tr, htr, dc] over ch 4 lp * around.

Rnd 8: * Working behind petals ch 5, sl st between 2 petals * around. (8 loops).

Rnd 9: Sl st into first lp. Ch 2 (counts as first tr). * 7 tr in each lp * around. Join.

Rnd 10: Ch 2 (counts as first tr). * Tr * around. Join. Insert mould.

Rnds 11, 12: * Dc in every other st * around. Fasten off.

The covered button former is inserted on Rnd 10. Rnds 11 and 12 close the crochet around the button.

(For additional help with this project, see Using Self-Cover Button Moulds, *page 10.*)

OPPOSITE: *These cotton Irish rose buttons have a homespun charm; make them more grown-up by using silk fabric and thread. For larger buttons, simply add more rounds of crochet.*

wool buttons

Buttons can be made from wool that has been spun, or remains unspun (fleece). The wool can be formed into a button on its own, or it can be wrapped or woven around a mould. Not surprisingly, wool buttons look particularly good on knitwear and woollen fabrics.

making a felt ball button

These are easy to make from fleece. If you are going to make several ball buttons, divide the fleece into equal sections before you begin.

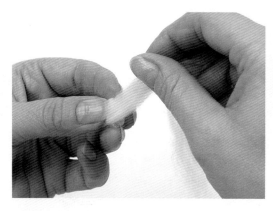

1. Tie a knot at the end of a length of fleece and wrap the wool around the knot to make a tight, even ball. Make the ball at least twice as big as the intended final size because it will shrink considerably.

2. Fill a bowl with hot water and dissolve plenty of soapflakes in it (soap helps to matt the fleece into felt). Use a spoon to dip the ball into the soapy water, then take it out again. Squeeze the ball to encourage the water to penetrate it fully. Dip and squeeze the ball again.

3. Roll the ball between your palms, gently at first, then increase the pressure as the fibres begin to matt together. Repeat the dipping, squeezing and rolling process until the ball is the required size. Rinse out the soap and place the ball on paper towels to dry, turning it regularly. Place it near a radiator to speed up the drying process.

It is important to check that the ball is fully shrunk and the fleece properly felted; this makes for a more durable button and provides the best surface for decorating. A good way to test this is to throw the ball hard on to a tabletop. The ball will bounce when fully felted.

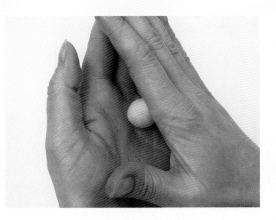

Attach felt ball buttons by sewing securely through the lower section of the ball.

making a pompom button

Pompoms can be made from any thickness of yarn; thick yarn will mean the wrapping process is quicker. Cut out two circles of thin card, each with a diameter of 4cm (1½in). Using small scissors, cut a circle with a diameter of 1.5cm (½in) out of the centre of each disc.

1. Hold the two discs together, trapping one end of the yarn under your finger. Pass the other end of the yarn through the central hole and continue to wrap it around the discs. Repeat the process until the discs are evenly covered in yarn. (If you wish, you can use more than one colour of yarn.)

2. Holding the discs very firmly at the centre, push the point of a pair of small, sharp scissors carefully between the two discs. Work the scissors around the edge of the pompom, keeping the blade between the discs and cutting through the strands of yarn.

3. Cut a new, generous length of yarn from the remainder of the ball. Using it double, tie a slip knot. Gently part the discs a little and put the loop between them and around the centre of the pompom. Tighten the slip knot until the pompom is secured, then pull away the discs. Trim off any uneven ends (but leave the ends of the slip knot – these can be used to attach the pompom to the garment or project).

useful tip
- If you are using an alternative yarn of a different weight it will be necessary to make a test pompom. The pompom should not be too dense or it will not pass easily through the button hole. Be sure to keep a note of the length of the yarn that you start with so that you can accurately repeat the process adding or decreasing the yarn as necessary to make the pompom more or less dense and so that you are able to create a number of similar pompoms if required.

making a yarn-covered button

This button is made on a clear plastic, loom-type mould. These are available from haberdashery stores in different sizes. Thread two tapestry needles, each with a different colour of yarn (use a generous length of each yarn as it is preferable for it to be continuous). The two colours are worked alternately.

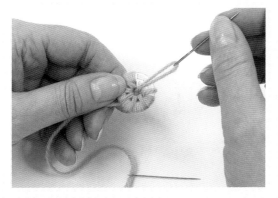

1. Work the first length of yarn over the outer rings of the mould: bring the needle through from back to front, holding the end of the yarn in place at the rear. (Work over the end with subsequent wraps to secure it.) Take the yarn to the back and pass it through the mould again, aligning the wrap with the previous one. Work four wraps, finishing at the back. Do not cut the yarn at this stage.

2. The second yarn is worked over the whole mould. Bring the needle to the front through the centre of the button, then make two wraps. Pick up the needle with the first yarn and bring it through to the front, twisting it around the second yarn to bring it back into the work.

3. Repeat the pattern of four wraps in the first colour, then two wraps in the second colour, all the way around the mould, keeping the wraps aligned, even and taut. To finish, weave in the ends on the back of the button.

felt ball button

Felt ball buttons are surprisingly quick and satisfying to make. Here, the whimsical effect has been heightened by the addition of tiny, pastel-coloured sequins and beads.

Materials

Fleece: small quantity of cream

Sequins: tiny flowers, pastel shades

Seed beads: in shades of pink

White beading thread

Soapflakes

Paper towels

Tools

Bowl of hot water and a spoon

Beading needle

1. Tie a knot at the end of a length of fleece and wrap the wool around the knot to make a tight, even ball. Make the ball at least twice as big as the intended final size because it will shrink considerably.

2. Fill a bowl with hot water and dissolve plenty of soapflakes in it (soap helps to matt the fleece into felt). Use a spoon to dip the ball into the soapy water, then take it out again. Squeeze the ball to encourage the water to penetrate it fully. Dip and squeeze the ball again.

3. Roll the ball between your palms, gently at first, then increase the pressure as the fibres begin to matt together. Repeat the dipping, squeezing and rolling process until the ball is the required size. Rinse out the soap and place the ball on paper towels to dry, turning it regularly. Leave it near a radiator to speed up the drying process.

4. Thread the beading needle with a long length of beading thread, knotted at the end. Starting at what will be the base of the button, pass the needle right through the button to what will be the centre top position. Thread a sequin and a seed bead on to the needle. Pass the needle back through the sequin so the bead will anchor it in place, then pass the needle back through the ball to emerge in the position of the next sequin. Repeat the process, leaving the base of the button free of decoration. See also Making a Felt Ball Button, *page 28.*)

OPPOSITE: *Instead of sequins, felt ball buttons could also be decorated with fabric dye pens; or try layering different colours of fleece as you wrap the ball, to get a marbled effect.*

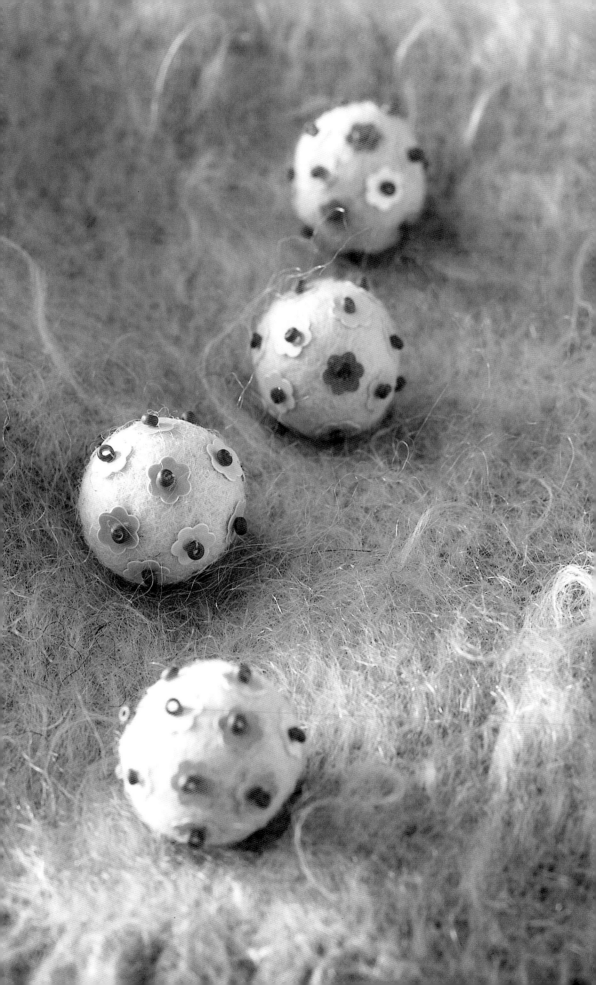

pompom button

Pompoms make a fun closure for children's clothing or accessories. For a perfectly coordinated finish, make them in a yarn to match the garment; for maximum impact use a contrasting yarn.

Materials

4-ply yarn: multicoloured

Tools

Thin card: 2 × circles, 4cm (1½in) in diameter, with a hole 1.5cm (½in) in diameter cut out of the centre of each

Small, sharp scissors

1. Cut off approximately 10m (11yds) of yarn for each pompom. If you wish to make several pompoms, it is important to use about the same length of yarn each time so that the finished pompoms will be of equal density.

2. Hold the two card discs together, trapping one end of the yarn under your finger. Pass the other end of the yarn through the central hole and continue to wrap it around the discs. Repeat the process until the discs are evenly covered in yarn.

3. Holding the discs very firmly at the centre, push the point of the scissors carefully between the two discs. Work the scissors around the edge of the pompom, keeping the blade between the discs and cutting through the strands of yarn.

4. Cut a new, generous length of yarn from the remainder of the ball. Using it double, tie a slip knot. Gently part the discs a little and put the loop between them and around the centre of the pompom. Tighten the slip knot until the pompom is secured, then pull away the discs. Trim off any uneven ends (but leave the ends of the slip knot to attach the pompom to the garment). For additional help with this project, refer to Making a Pompom Button, *page 29-30*.

OPPOSITE: *These jolly pompoms coordinate perfectly with the stripy hand knit. Make the pompoms larger or smaller by adjusting the size of the discs. The more wraps you make, the denser the pompom will be, but avoid making them too dense or they will be difficult to fit through a buttonhole.*

yarn-covered button

These cartwheel-effect buttons look especially good on knitted or woollen garments. Yarn can be woven around the purchased moulds in a variety of ways to give different results: see the diagrams on the pack. Try experimenting with various colours and textures of yarn.

Materials

Tapestry wool: soft green and soft blue

Tools

Plastic loom-type moulds: 22mm (⅞in) in diameter, quantity as desired

Tapestry needles: 2

Scissors

1. Thread one tapestry needle with green yarn and the other with blue yarn (use a generous length of each as it is preferable for the yarn to be continuous). The two colours are worked alternately.

2. Work the green yarn over the outer rings of the mould: bring the needle through from back to front, holding the end of the yarn securely at the rear. (Work over the end with subsequent wraps to secure it.) Take the yarn to the back and pass it through the mould again, aligning the wrap with the previous one. Work four wraps, finishing at the back. Do not cut the yarn at this stage.

3. Work the blue yarn over the whole mould. Bring the needle to the front through the centre of the button, then make two wraps. Pick up the needle with the green yarn and bring it through to the front, twisting it around the blue yarn to bring it back into work.

4. Repeat the pattern of four wraps in green, then two wraps in blue, all the way around the mould, keeping the wraps aligned, even and taut. To finish, weave in the ends on the back of the button. (For additional help with this project, see Making a Yarn-Covered Button, *page 31*.)

OPPOSITE: *The soft colours of these yarn-covered buttons harmonize well with the muted tartan that they have been applied to. For subtle interest, the colours have been worked in opposite ways. Tapestry wool is available in a wonderful range of colours; alternatively, 4-ply wool can be used.*

beaded buttons

Beads come in an endless range of sizes, shapes and colours, but smaller ones are particularly well suited to decorating buttons. The look of the finished buttons will depend on the type of beads used.

making a beaded toggle

The toggle is covered by winding a string of beads around it. For the neatest effect, keep the spiral of beads as even as possible, and make sure that the pattern remains unbroken either side of the screw eye used to sew the button to the garment or project.

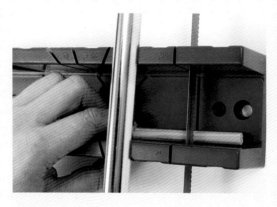

1. First, cut a piece of wooden dowel to the required length – about 3.5cm (1⅜in) – by placing it in a mitre block and using a saw. Sand the ends smooth and paint the dowel (use acrylic spray paint, ensuring that all manufacturer's recommendations are observed).

2. Find the centre of the dowel and make a small pilot hole, then twist in a small screw eye. Make a pilot hole in the centre of each end and push a domed upholstery nail into each one.

3. Thread a beading needle with beading thread (leaving it attached to the reel) and string the beads.

5. Tie the end of the beading thread nearest the needle around the upholstery nail and spread a little superglue near the end of the dowel. Wrap the strung beads around the glued dowel, making sure that they sit parallel with (and snugly against) the edge of the upholstery nail.

6. Spiral the strung beads along the dowel, applying more superglue as required. When you reach the screw eye, part the beads so that they fit around it. When you come to the end, ensure that the beads sit close to the edge of the upholstery nail, wrap the thread around the nail and tie it off to secure it. Trim off the remaining thread.

4. Using the length of the needle to measure when to change bead colour, pick up a needle full of the first colour of bead, followed by the second colour and then the third colour. Repeat until the string is approximately 70cm (27½in) long.

making a beaded button

These beaded buttons are worked on a purchased button mould covered in silk fabric. The fabric is stretched in an embroidery hoop for the initial beading to take place. When the button has been covered, the final beading is applied.

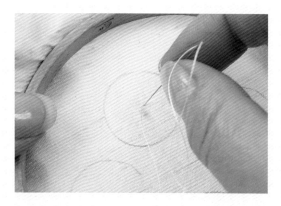

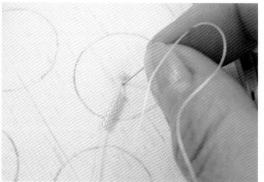

1. Fit the fabric into a small embroidery hoop. Place the button size guide on the fabric and draw around it with a fabric marker. You will be able to fit several circles within the hoop, so a number of buttons can be worked on together.

Thread a beading needle with a length of beading thread and knot one end. Bring the needle up through the centre of one of the drawn circles and pick up a bead. Take the needle back down close to where it came out.

2. Bring the needle back up through the fabric to one side of the bead, and pick up 7 beads. Take the needle back down through the fabric exactly where it came out, and pull gently to tighten the loop of beads.

3. Position the loop of beads over the central bead. Bring the needle up through the fabric, just inside the loop. Make a stitch over the loop, pulling it tight so that it slips between two beads and holds the loop in place. Repeat the process at every alternate bead to attach the whole loop.

Follow steps 1–3 again, but this time picking up 14 beads, to make a second loop of beads around the first one. Secure the thread at the back of the fabric. Cover the button following the instructions for Using a Self-Cover Button Mould on page 10. Leave a long end of thread and ensure that this is trapped between the back and front of the button when the button is assembled.

4. Thread the long end of thread into a beading needle and make a tiny stitch through the fabric to bring the needle out on the rim of the button. Pick up a bead and make a small backstitch through the fabric to attach it, then bring the needle out further along the button rim, ready for the next bead.

Repeat the process to attach an evenly spaced ring of beads right around the edge of the button. Secure the thread on the fabric close to the back of the button.

useful tips
- All beads have a number that reflects their size. The larger the number the smaller the bead, so a 6 is quite large and a 12 is tiny. Seed beads are generally considered to be size 11 or 12.
- Not all beads are washable so it is generally best to remove beaded buttons before laundering.

beaded toggle

Metallic beads in subtly graduated shades give these toggles a sophisticated look that belies the straightforward materials and techniques used to make them.

Materials

Wooden dowel: 3.5cm (1⅜in) × 9mm (⅜in) in diameter, per toggle

Matt acrylic spray paint, black

Upholstery nails, bronzed: 2 × 13mm (½in) per toggle

Screw eye: 1 × 5mm (³⁄₁₆in) in diameter, per toggle

Beading thread

Glass beads: 2-cut, size 15, in pewter, light and dark bronze

Superglue

Tools

Saw and mitre box; sandpaper

Ruler, pencil and scissors

Multitool fitted with a 1mm (¹⁄₃₂in) HSS drill bit

Beading needle

1. For each toggle, cut a piece of dowel 3.5cm (1⅜in) long by placing it in the mitre block and using the saw. Sand the ends smooth and paint the dowel black.

2. Make pilot holes in the centre and each end of the dowel with the multitool. Insert the screw eye in the centre hole and push an upholstery nail into each end.

3. Thread the beading needle with beading thread (leaving it attached to the reel) and string the beads. Using the length of the needle to measure when to change bead colour, pick up a needle full of pewter beads, followed by light bronze beads and then dark bronze beads. Repeat until the string is approximately 70cm (27½in) long.

4. Tie the needle end of the beading thread around the upholstery nail and spread a little superglue near the end of the dowel. Wrap the strung beads around the glued dowel, making sure that they sit parallel with, (and snugly against) the edge of the upholstery nail.

5. Spiral the strung beads along the dowel, applying more superglue as required. When you reach the screw eye, part the beads so that they fit around it. At the other end, ensure that the beads sit close to the edge of the upholstery nail, wrap the thread around the nail and tie it off to secure it. Trim off the remaining thread. (See also Making a Beaded Toggle, *page 38-9*.)

OPPOSITE: *Flat-sided beads work especially well for this technique, tending to align themselves more easily. Match upholstery nails to your beads by painting them with enamel paint if necessary.*

beaded button

These pretty, pearl-encrusted buttons are tiny enough to be used closely spaced on a wedding gown. Ring the changes by making them in sophisticated black for evening, or in bright colours for a fun, contemporary look.

Materials

Dupion silk fabric: cream

Beading thread: white

Pearl seed beads: size 10

Self-cover buttons: quantity as required × 11mm (⁷⁄₁₆in) in diameter

Tools

Small embroidery hoop

Fabric marker

Beading needle

Small, sharp scissors

1. Fit the fabric into the embroidery hoop. Using the button size guide, draw several circles with the fabric marker so a number of buttons can be worked on together. Thread the beading needle with a length of beading thread and knot one end. Bring the needle up through the centre of a circle and pick up a bead. Take the needle back down close to where it came out. Bring the needle back up, to one side of the bead, and pick up 7 beads. Take the needle back down exactly where it came out, and pull gently to tighten the loop of beads. Position the loop of beads over the central bead. Bring the needle up just inside the loop. Make a stitch over the loop, pulling it tight so that it slips between two beads and holds the loop in place. Repeat at every alternate bead to attach the whole loop.

2. Follow step 1 again, this time with 14 beads, to make a second loop of beads around the first one. Leave a long end of thread to trap between the back and front of the button. Assemble the button. Thread the long end of thread into a beading needle and bring it out on the rim of the button. Pick up a bead and make a small backstitch to attach it, then bring the needle out further along the button rim, ready for the next bead. Repeat the process to attach an evenly spaced ring of beads around the edge of the button. Secure the thread. (See also Making a Beaded Button, *page 40-1*.)

OPPOSITE: *The finished buttons. Make bigger buttons by using a larger button-former and working additional loops with more beads each time. Line the former if the fabric is fine or sheer.*

embroidered buttons

Simple hand and machine embroidery techniques can be used to create an infinite range of buttons with a tactile quality.

hand embroidering a daisy

A daisy is made up of single chain stitches arranged in a circle. The size and the number of petals can be varied to suit the button-former.

1. Fit the fabric into a small embroidery hoop. Draw round the button size guide on the fabric, as in Step 1, page 40. Thread a needle with embroidery thread and knot one end. Bring the needle up through the centre of a circle. Take the needle back down close to where it came out, leaving a small loop on the face of the work. To form the first petal, bring the needle up through the fabric and the loop, a short distance away. Pull gently to tension the loop, and make a small stitch to secure it by passing the needle back down through the fabric. Bring the needle back up through the centre of the circle and repeat the process until the desired number of petals have been formed. Secure the thread on the back of the fabric. Trim off the end.

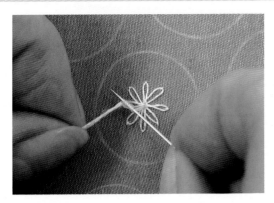

2. To make a French knot in the centre of the daisy, thread a needle with embroidery thread and bring the needle up through the centre of the motif. Wrap the thread around the needle a number of times, keeping the point of the needle close to the spot where it emerged, and the thread taut.

3. Pass the needle back through the fabric near the point it emerged and pull through the thread; a small knot will form on the surface of the fabric. Secure the thread on the back of the fabric and trim off the end.

hand embroidering an initial

This technique uses cellulose thinners to transfer a photocopied letter onto the fabric. Reverse the photocopy so that the letter appears backwards. The letter is then embroidered with a combination of stitches.

1. To transfer the letter on to the fabric, dip the tip of a cotton bud into cellulose thinners and wipe it over the back of the reversed image to loosen the ink. As you wipe on the cellulose thinners, the letter will become visible through the paper. (Observe the manufacturer's precautions when using cellulose thinners, and avoid contact with the skin.)

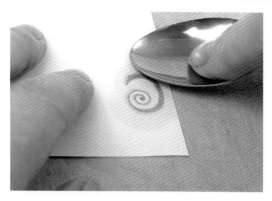

2. To transfer the print to the fabric, place the print in position, face down. Rub firmly, all over the back, with the bowl of a metal spoon. Hold the print securely while you are rubbing so that it does not move and smudge the ink. Carefully lift off the print.

3. Fit the fabric into a small embroidery hoop. Thread an embroidery needle with embroidery thread and tie a knot in the end. Work a small backstitch around the outer edge of the letter. Where the letterform is thin, the backstitch will remain visible on the completed letter.

4. On the areas where the letterform is thickest, work a satin stitch across the lines of backstitch, starting and ending each stitch just to the outer edges of the backstitch. For best results, keep the stitches aligned and level, and the embroidery thread smooth. This letter is finished with a French knot: see the instructions for Embroidering a Daisy, *page 47*. Secure the thread on the back of the fabric and trim off the end.

machine embroidering concentric circles

To ensure that the machine embroidery is only worked on the face of the button, use the front of the self-cover button as a template. This way the embroidered fabric will still fit over a self-cover button mould.

1. Fit the fabric into a small embroidery hoop. Using a fabric marker, draw around the front of the self-cover button to make a template for the stitching.

2. Set up the sewing machine for free-machine embroidery and stitch embroidered circles within the marked area. Change colour as required.

machine embroidering a punched motif

Paddle punches, used for papercrafts, are great for punching shapes out of non-fray fabrics such as felt or leather. If you are embroidering on to a fine or stretchy fabric, work with a layer of stable fabric, such as lightweight cotton, underneath. Fit the two fabrics into the embroidery hoop together.

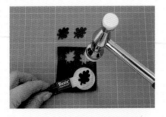

1. Working on a self-healing mat, use a paddle punch and hammer to punch a shape out of a scrap of fabric.

2. Place the motif in position. With the sewing machine set up for free-machine embroidery, embroider detail on the motif.

embroidered daisy button

These little buttons, with a sweet, hand-embroidered daisy motif, are a simple way to freshen up an everyday shirt.

Materials

Green cotton shirting fabric

Stranded embroidery cotton: oddments of white and yellow

Self-cover buttons: quantity as required × 11mm (⅞₆in) in diameter

Tools

Small embroidery hoop

Fabric marker

Embroidery needle

Small, sharp scissors

1. Fit the fabric into the embroidery hoop. Place the button size guide on the fabric and draw around it with the fabric marker. Draw several circles to work on.

2. Thread the needle with a single strand of white thread and knot one end. Bring the needle up through the centre of one of the circles. Take the needle back down close to where it came out, leaving a small loop on the face of the work. To form the first petal, bring the needle up through the fabric and the loop, 4mm (³⁄₁₆in) away. Pull gently to tension the loop, and make a small stitch to secure it by passing the needle back down through the fabric. Bring the needle back up through the centre of the circle and repeat the process to make a total of 8 petals. Secure the thread on the back of the fabric and trim off the end.

3. To make a French knot in the centre of the daisy, thread the needle with three strands of yellow thread and bring it up through the centre of the daisy. Wrap the thread around the needle three times, keeping the point of the needle close to the spot where it emerged and the thread taut. Pass the needle back through the fabric near the point it emerged and a small knot will form. Secure the thread on the back of the fabric. Cover the button mould in the usual way. (See also Hand Embroidering a Daisy, *page 46-7*, and Using Self-Cover Button Moulds, *page 10*.)

OPPOSITE: *A store-bought shirt can look great with replacement buttons; just be sure to coordinate the fabrics carefully to ensure that the buttons are in keeping with the garment.*

embroidered initial button

This technique uses cellulose thinners to transfer a reversed photocopied letter onto fabric ready for embroidery. Choose a font that is not too complex.

Materials

Ecru linen fabric

Stranded embroidery thread: oddments of dull red

Cellulose thinners

Self-cover buttons: quantity as required × 22mm (⅞in) in diameter

Tools

Reversed photocopied letters

Cotton bud; spoon

Small embroidery hoop

Embroidery needle

Small, sharp scissors

1. Dip the tip of a cotton bud into cellulose thinners and wipe it over the back of the reversed photocopied image. As you wipe on the cellulose thinners, the letter will become visible through the paper.

2. To transfer the print to the fabric, place the print in position, face down. Rub firmly with a metal spoon. Hold the print securely while you are rubbing so that it does not move and smudge the ink. Carefully lift off the print.

3. Fit the fabric into the embroidery hoop. Thread the needle with thread and tie a knot in the end. Work a small backstitch around the outer edge of the letter. Where the letterform is thin, the backstitch will remain visible. On the areas where the letterform is thickest, work a satin stitch across the lines of backstitch, starting and ending each stitch just to the outer edges of the backstitch. This letter is finished with a French knot: see the instructions for Embroidering a Daisy, *page 46-7*. Secure the thread on the back of the fabric. Cover the button mould in the usual way. (See also Hand Embroidering an Initial, *page 47*, and Using Self-Cover Button Moulds, *page 10*.)

OPPOSITE: *The technique used for transferring the letters gives a clear and accurate shape for you to stitch around. Cellulose thinners can be harmful if safety precautions are not observed, so be sure to read the manufacturer's instructions and safety directions carefully.*

shisha mirror button

These buttons are completely covered in stitch and have a lovely texture; the smooth shine of the mirror provides an interesting contrast. Shisha mirrors are traditional in Indian embroidery.

Materials

Red felt (with a layer of cotton fabric underneath for support)

Machine embroidery thread: variegated pink, orange and cranberry

Pink shisha mirrors: quantity as for number of buttons

Sewing thread: red and pink

Self-cover buttons: quantity as required × 29mm (1⅛in) in diameter

Tools

Sewing machine

Small, sharp scissors

Small embroidery hoop

Hand-sewing needle

Fabric marker

1. Fit the fabric into a small embroidery hoop. To ensure that the machine embroidery is only worked on the face of the button, use the front of the self-cover button as a template. Draw around it with the fabric marker.

2. Set up the sewing machine for free-machine embroidery, with cranberry embroidery thread on the top and red sewing thread on the bobbin. Stitch concentric circles within the marked area, entirely covering the surface of the felt so that it cannot be seen through the stitches. Work approximately two-thirds of the way across the circle, changing the colour of the embroidery thread as required. Do not embroider the centre section of the circle as this will later be concealed by a shisha mirror. Trim away the cotton fabric from the back, close to the edge of the stitching, and trim off any ends.

3. Cover the button mould in the usual way. To finish the button, thread a hand-sewing needle with pink thread and sew the shisha mirror securely in place at the centre of the button. Trim off any ends. (For additional help with this project, refer to Machine Embroidering Concentric Circles, page 49, and Using Self-Cover Button Moulds, page 10.)

OPPOSITE: *Used on garments or furnishings, these splendid buttons are sure to catch the eye. Make the set subtly dissimilar by working the colours in a different order.*

leather leaf button

The rich colours and textures of these classy suede and leather buttons lend them an opulent appeal, which is certain to enhance a variety of projects.

Materials

Brown leather: oddments

Purple suede with a layer of cotton fabric underneath for support

Metallic embroidery thread: copper

Sewing thread: brown

Seed beads: bronze

Beading thread: brown

Self-cover buttons: quantity as required × 29mm (1⅛in) in diameter

Tools

Leaf motif paddle punch; hammer

Self-healing mat

Sewing machine; scissors

Embroidery hoop; beading needle

1. Working on the self-healing mat, use the paddle punch and hammer to punch a leaf shape out of the brown leather. Fit the purple suede (with the cotton underneath) into the embroidery hoop and position the leaf motif on it.

2. Set up the sewing machine for free-machine embroidery, with copper embroidery thread on the top and brown sewing thread on the bobbin. Work backwards and forwards to embroider veins on the leaf. Trim off any ends.

3. Thread the beading needle with beading thread and tie a knot in the end. Sew the seed beads to the tip of the veins in a random pattern, using 4 or 5 beads per leaf. Secure the thread on the back of the work and trim off the end. Cover the button mould in the usual way. (For additional help with this project, refer to Machine Embroidering a Punched Motif, *page 49*, and Using Self-Cover Button Moulds, *page 10*.)

OPPOSITE: *Leather is a great material for punching shapes out of, as the edges won't fray. The suede surfaces help to keep the motif in position as you sew, avoiding the need for glue.*

clay buttons

Both polymer clay and air-drying clay can be used to create buttons of diverse character. Polymer clay is available in a range of colours; air-drying clay can be painted when dry.

making a millefiore flower cane

Use polymer clay for this fantastic technique, which takes a little time and practice but is well worth the effort involved. For even faster results, buy ready-made millefiore canes.

1. Knead the clay, then roll it into a sausage shape using a piece of acrylic. Roll one yellow sausage 1cm (⅜in) in diameter and five white sausages 1.5cm (½in) in diameter. All should be the same length.

2. To form the flower, pinch evenly all along one side of each white sausage to create a petal shape. Arrange the white petals evenly around the yellow centre.

3. Prepare five blue sausages the same size and shape as the white ones. Wedge them between the white petal-shaped sausages and squeeze to fix the shape. Roll out a thin slab of blue clay and wrap it around the flower. Trim it to fit, and seal the edges by smoothing them with your thumb.

4. Reduce the size of the basic flower cane by rolling it gently with the piece of acrylic. Every so often, squeeze along the cane and lightly stretch it to help stop it from splitting. As the cane lengthens, the ends will become concave. Trim them with a craft knife, and check for splits in the clay before continuing the reduction process. Produce seven canes about 8mm (5⁄16in) in diameter. All should be of equal length.

5. Roll a blue sausage, 1cm (3⁄8in) in diameter, to the same length as the reduced canes, and arrange the reduced canes around it. Roll out a thin slab of blue clay and wrap it around the canes, trimming and sealing as before. Roll the cane a little more to consolidate the clay and achieve the desired finished size.

6. Use a blade from a craft knife to cut the cane into even slices, approximately 4mm (³⁄₁₆in) thick. Reshape the slices to make the discs circular, for the final buttons.

7. Use a darning needle to make two holes in each button, near the centre and within the blue area. Ensure that the holes are big enough for thread or yarn to pass through.

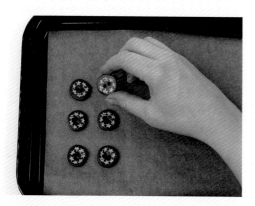

8. To harden the clay, place the buttons on a baking tray lined with baking parchment, and bake them according to the clay manufacturer's instructions.

Shaping polymer clay with cutters

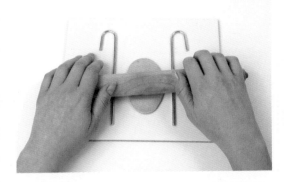

1. Knead the clay and roll it out, resting the rolling pin on two matching implements such as metal tent pegs. This will ensure that the clay is rolled to an even thickness.

2. Dip a cutter in a little water and press it firmly into the clay. Gently push the shape out of the cutter: the water will help to ensure that it is released easily.

Using a press-mould with air-drying clay

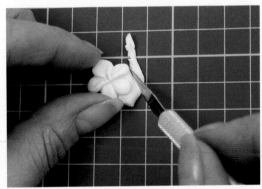

1. Spray the mould with a little lubricant. Knead a small amount of clay then press it firmly into the mould (it should overlap the edge a little). Holding the excess clay, very gently pull the shape out of the mould.

2. Place the clay shape on a cutting mat and using a craft knife, carefully trim away the excess clay around the edge of the shape. Allow to dry and paint as required.

millefiore button

'Millefiore' is an Italian word meaning 'thousand flowers'. The process of making polymer clay canes is very therapeutic. The canes can be worked in many ways to create intricate and interesting buttons. Watching the image in a large cane shrink into miniature is a delight.

Materials

Yellow polymer clay: 1 block

White polymer clay: 1 block

Marine blue polymer clay: 2 blocks

Tools

Piece of acrylic

Rolling pin

Smooth tile

Ruler

Blade from a craft knife

Darning needle

Baking paper and baking tray

Oven

1. Knead all the clay, then prepare the flower cane following the instructions given on *page 58-9*. Produce seven reduced canes, 8mm (⅜in) in diameter and about 5cm (2in) long.

2. The buttons have a plain blue centre to accommodate the holes for stitching through. To create this, roll a blue sausage, 1cm (⅜in) in diameter and 5cm (2in) long, then arrange the reduced canes around it. Use the rolling pin to roll out a thin slab of blue clay and wrap it around the canes, trimming and sealing as before. Consolidate the clay by rolling it into a cane 2.5cm (1in) in diameter.

3. Use the blade to cut the cane into even slices approximately 4mm (⅜in) thick. Reshape the slices into discs. Make two holes in each disc with the darning needle, near the centre and within the blue area. Ensure that the holes are big enough for sewing thread or yarn to pass through. Bake the buttons according to the manufacturer's instructions. (For additional help with this project, see Making a Millefiore Flower Cane, *page 58-60*.)

OPPOSITE: *These buttons demonstrate how a number of straightforward flower canes can be used, but once you have mastered the technique it is possible to create amazingly intricate patterns and even pictures within the canes.*

letter button

Any young girl would covet these fun buttons made from glittery polymer clay and studded with gems for extra sparkle.

Materials

Polymer clay: 1 block containing silver glitter

Silver gems: 3mm (⅛in) in diameter, number as required

Superglue

Tools

Rolling pin and smooth tile

Metal tent pegs (or other matching items): 2, approximately 4mm (³⁄₁₆in) thick

Shallow dish of water

Darning needle

Pricking pad or mouse mat

Baking paper and baking tray

3cm letter cutters

Oven

1. Knead the clay and roll it out on a smooth tile. To ensure you roll the clay to an even thickness, use the tent pegs to rest the rolling pin on as you work. The rolled clay should be about 4mm (³⁄₁₆in) thick.

2. Dip a cutter in a little water and cut out a shape by pressing the cutter firmly through the clay. Gently push the letter shape out of the cutter; the water will help to ensure that it is released easily.

3. Place the letter on the pricking pad or mouse mat to prevent it from distorting, and use the darning needle to make two sewing holes in an appropriate position. (This will vary according to the letter.) Gently press a gem into the surface of the letter, in the desired position, making a small indentation to identify the spot. Remove the gem for the baking process.

4. Bake the button according to the manufacturer's instructions. When the button has cooled, glue the gem in position. (For additional help with this project, refer to Shaping Polymer Clay wih Cutters, *page 61*.)

OPPOSITE: *Although adult supervision would be required for the baking process, these buttons are so simple that a young child could make them. There are many shaped cutters available; you can use those that are designed especially for use with clay, or alternatively, baking or aspic cutters.*

violet button

Pearlescent paint gives these violet buttons a really special finish, reminiscent of shot silk. They would make a pretty fastening for an evening gown or a piece of delicate knitwear.

Materials

Air-drying clay: white

Acrylic paint: pearlescent violet

Fine felt-tipped pen: purple

Sunflower oil spray

Tools

Press-mould with violet flower shape

Craft knife

Cutting mat

Darning needle

Pricking pad or mouse mat

Fine paintbrush

1. Spray the mould with a little lubricant so that the clay shape will be released more easily. Knead a small amount of clay then press it firmly into the mould (it should overlap the edge a little). Holding the excess clay, very gently pull the shape out of the mould.

2. Place the clay shape on the cutting mat and using the craft knife, carefully trim away the excess clay around the edge of the shape. Smooth any uneven edges with your finger.

3. Place the clay violet face up on the pricking pad to prevent it distorting. Use the darning needle to make two holes near the centre of the flower. These are the stitching holes, so ensure that they are large enough for sewing thread to pass through. Allow the clay to dry thoroughly.

4. Paint the violet with the pearlescent paint, mixing it with a little water if necessary. Allow the paint to dry. To finish the button and add extra dimension, use the felt-tipped pen to darken the creases and folds of the petals. (For additional help with this project, refer to Using a Press-Mould on Air-Drying Clay, *page 61*.)

OPPOSITE: *The finished violets have a subtle gleam. Push-moulds for many motifs are available. For the best results when making buttons, choose small shapes that are not too deep. As well as their conventional use on a garment, these buttons make pretty embellishments for cards and craft projects.*

found-item buttons

Techniques will vary depending on the materials being used, but half the fun in creating buttons from found items and unconventional objects is finding a way to make them work.

drilling a shell

Whole shells, or pieces of broken shell, can be used to make buttons. Both are very brittle and require careful drilling. A sharp drill bit and practice are necessary, but expect to break a fair percentage!

Fit a multitool with a small HSS drill bit. Rest the shell on a piece of scrap wood, supporting it with a small piece of modelling clay. Drill steadily and avoid putting too much pressure on the shell as you work. Repeat to drill the second hole.

using a bottletop to make a funky frame

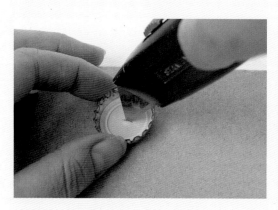

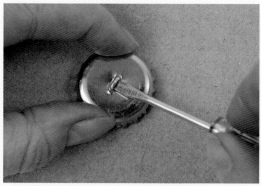

1. Use a craft knife to cut a small slot in the centre of a bottletop. Use the tip of a flat screwdriver to make the slot large enough to accommodate the shank of a plain, flat metal button.

2. Locate the shank in the slot and push the button into place inside the bottletop. On the outside, use the screwdriver to work the metal back down around the shank to hold the button in place.

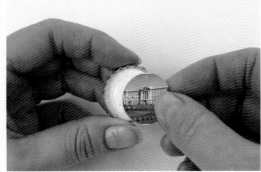

3. Punch an image out of glossy, coated paper: a postcard is ideal. The diameter of the image must be about the same as that of the bottletop.

4. Fill the edges between the button and the bottletop with PVA glue, allowing it to spread over the button. Place the image in the bottletop, aligning vertically with the shank. Leave to dry (keep level).

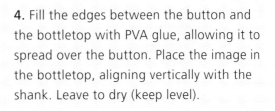

5. Seal the edge between the image and the bottletop with glitter glue. Make sure it's a good seal. Allow it to dry.

6. Draw crystal resin into a syringe, then fill the bottletop almost to the top, covering the image. Leave it flat to dry .

shell button

These buttons are made from fragments of much larger shells, worn smooth by the sea. Go beachcombing at the next opportunity to find natural treasures of your own.

Materials

Fragments of shells

Fine silver jewellery wire

Superglue

Modelling clay: small piece

Tools

Multitool fitted with a 1.5mm (¹⁄₁₆in) HSS drill bit

Piece of scrap wood

Jewellery wire cutters and pliers

1. Fit the multitool with the drill bit. Rest the shell on a piece of scrap wood, supporting it with a small piece of modelling clay. Drill steadily and avoid putting too much pressure on the shell as you work. Repeat the process to drill a second hole 6mm (¼in) away.

2. Cut a length of jewellery wire and wrap it tightly around the shell, in between the holes. Make four or five wraps and then use the pliers to twist the ends of the wire securely together on the back of the button. Trim off the ends of the wire. Press the twist flat against the back of the button, making sure that the end is well tucked in. To ensure that the wires stay in place, secure them with a little superglue on the back of the button.

3. When you come to sew the buttons on to the project, sew the yarn over the top of the wrapped wires.
(For additional help with this project, refer to Drilling a Shell, *page 68.*)

OPPOSITE: *These shell buttons, with their subtle shades and patterns and fine wire detailing, have been used to decorate the edge of a mohair wrap. The contrasting textures are very pleasing to look at and also to touch.*

bottletop button

These fun, kitsch buttons contain a miniature image preserved under resin. Postcards are highly suited to this treatment, due to the availability of small-scale images and the glossy finish of the card, which prevents the resin from soaking through it.

Materials

Bottletops: number as required

Plain, flat metal button with a shank: 18mm ($\frac{11}{16}$in) in diameter, number as required

Postcard(s)

PVA glue

Glitter glue: red and rainbow

Crystal resin

Tools

Craft knife

Piece of scrap wood

Small, flat-ended screwdriver

Round craft punch

Syringe

1. Put the bottletop on the scrap wood and use the craft knife to cut a small slot in the centre. Use the tip of a flat screwdriver to make the slot large enough to accommodate the shank of the metal button.

2. Locate the shank in the slot and push the button into place inside the bottletop. On the outside, use the screwdriver to work the metal back down around the shank to hold the button in place.

3. Use the craft punch to punch an image out of the postcard, centring the main feature. The diameter of the image must be about the same as that of the bottletop.

4. Fill the edges between the button and the bottletop with PVA glue, allowing it to spread over the button. Place the image in the bottletop, aligning it vertically with the shank. Leave to dry (keep level).

5. Seal the edge between the image and the bottletop with glitter glue. Make sure it's a good seal. Allow to dry.

6. Mix the crystal resin with hardener according to the manufacturer's instructions. Draw some into a syringe and fill the bottletop almost to the top, covering the image. Leave it flat to dry. (For additional help with this project, see Using a Bottletop as a Funky Frame, *page 68-9*.)

OPPOSITE: *These amusing buttons preserve memories of a visit to London. You could also try embedding small items such as charms, coins or shells into the resin.*

wooden buttons

Wood can be used to make lovely buttons. Choose either prepared smoothed lengths or shaped pieces, or use wood it in its natural, rustic, bark-covered form.

using a twig to make a toggle

Twigs with a diameter of around 1cm (⅜in) are ideal for this technique, which can utilize waste wood in its natural state.

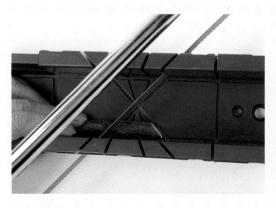

1. Place the twig in a mitre box and use a saw to cut the end at an angle of 45°. Mark a point 5cm (2in) along the twig. Put the twig back in the mitre box and cut the other end at an opposing 45° angle. The long side will measure 5cm (2in) and the short side will be 2.5cm (1in). If necessary, smooth the face of the cut edges using fine-grade sandpaper.

2. Using a craft knife, cut away a shallow section of bark approximately 1.5cm (½in) long, centred on the short face of the toggle. Sandpaper as before.

3. Using a drill fitted with a small drill bit and working on a piece of scrap wood, drill two holes, locating them centrally within the area cut away in step 2, approximately 8mm (⁵⁄₁₆in) apart.

4. Fit the drill with a countersink bit and shape each end of the first hole into a shallow cup. Repeat on the second hole.

making a button from a broom handle

A broom handle provides a piece of thick wooden dowel that will yield lots of buttons! A mitre box is used to cut elliptical shapes.

1. Place a broom handle in a mitre box and use a saw to cut the end at an angle of 45°. Mark a point 5mm (³⁄₁₆in) along the broom handle. Put the broom handle back in the mitre box and saw an elliptical slice of wood, 5mm (³⁄₁₆in) thick.

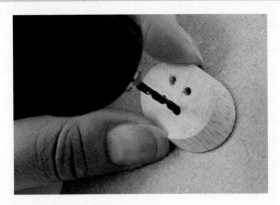

2. Put the slice of wood on a piece of scrap wood and use a drill fitted with a small drill bit to drill four holes that are centred within the ellipse. Smooth the surfaces of the button with fine-grade sandpaper.

3. Decorate the edge and the face of the button, using a pyrography tool to make different markings. Seal the finished button with two coats of matt acrylic varnish.

useful tips

- If you don't have a pyrography tool a soldering iron can be used to make simple marks which lend themselves well to the naive, rustic charm of these buttons.

- Cut the broom handle across at 90° to make more conventional round buttons.

covering a wooden shape with handmade paper

Purchased wooden shapes can be covered with handmade paper, resulting in a unique and attractive finish. Choose a soft, lightweight paper with long, flexible fibres, such as mulberry paper, for this technique.

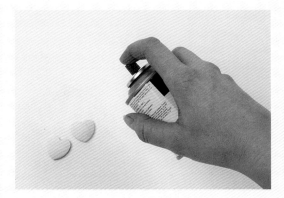

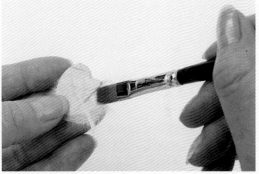

1. Put the wooden shape on a protected surface and spray the sides and the face evenly with spray paint (observe the manufacturer's safety directions). Allow it to dry, then turn it over and spray the back. Leave it to dry thoroughly.

2. Mix up a small amount of cellulose wallpaper paste according to the manufacturer's instructions. Using a flat brush, apply a layer of paste to the face and sides of the shape. Tear off a small piece of paper and apply it to the wooden shape, allowing it to wrap around the sides. Use more paste and the end of the brush to help mould the paper around the shape. Tear off another small piece of paper and apply it next to the first. The torn edges should slightly overlap, but they will not create a harsh line. Repeat the pasting and wrapping process until you have covered the entire shape. Allow it to dry thoroughly.

rustic toggle

Thick twigs with an attractive bark can be used to fashion unique toggles with a wonderful rustic appeal.

Materials

Twig(s): 1cm (⅜in) in diameter

Tools

Mitre box

Saw

Fine-grade sandpaper

Craft knife

Drill fitted with a 2mm (¹⁄₁₆in) HSS drill bit

Countersink drill bit

Piece of scrap wood

These toggles are best made from twigs of an even thickness with attractive bark, such as this cherry wood. Wipe twigs with a damp cloth to clean them before you start.

1. Place the twig in the mitre box and use the saw to cut the end at an angle of 45°. Mark a point 5cm (2in) along the twig. Put the twig back in the mitre box and cut the other end at an opposing 45° angle. The long side will measure 5cm (2in) and the short side will be 2.5cm (1in). If necessary, smooth the face of the cut edges with fine-grade sandpaper.

2. Using the craft knife, cut away a shallow section of bark approximately 1.5cm (½in) long, centred on the short face of the toggle. Sandpaper as before.

3. Working on a piece of scrap wood, drill two holes, locating them centrally within the area cut away in step 2, approximately 8mm (⁵⁄₁₆in) apart.

4. Fit the drill with the countersink bit and shape each end of the first hole into a shallow cup. Repeat on the second hole. (For additional help with this project, refer to Using a Twig to Make a Toggle, *page 74.*)

OPPOSITE: *These attractive toggles are easy to make from pruned branches. The irregularities in shape and unique markings in the wood contribute to their individual charm.*

pyrography button

Nobody will guess that these striking buttons have been made from a humble broom handle! The branded markings are made using a pyrography tool with different-shaped interchangeable tips.

Materials

Broom handle or wooden dowel: 24mm ($^{15}/_{16}$in) thick

Clear matt acrylic varnish

Tools

Mitre box

Saw

Ruler

Fine-grade sandpaper

Drill fitted with a 2.5mm ($^1/_{16}$in) HSS drill bit

Piece of scrap wood

Pyrography tool with interchangeable tips

Scrap paper to protect work surface

Small, flat paintbrush

Although the broom handle could easily be cut into circular discs, the result is a little more unusual when slices are cut at an angle.

1. Place the broom handle in the mitre box and use the saw to cut the end at an angle of 45°. Mark a point 5mm ($^3/_{16}$in) along the broom handle. Put the broom handle back in the mitre box and saw an elliptical slice of wood, 5mm ($^3/_{16}$in) thick.

2. Put the slice of wood on a piece of scrap wood and drill four holes that are centred within the ellipse. Smooth the surfaces of the button with fine-grade sandpaper.

3. Working on a heat-proof surface, decorate the edge and the face of the button, using the pyrography tool and a selection of tips to make different markings. (Remember to allow the tool to cool down completely before changing the tip.)

4. Working on a protected surface, seal the finished button with two coats of matt acrylic varnish. (For additional help with this project, refer to Making a Button from a Broom Handle, *page 75-6*.)

OPPOSITE: *Wooden dowel is available in a range of different diameters and could equally well be used to make buttons of this type; however for larger buttons, a broom handle makes a good and inexpensive alternative.*

heart-shaped wooden button

Pre-cut wooden shapes, in a variety of motifs, are widely available from craft shops. Here handmade mulberry paper containing different coloured fibres has given these wooden hearts an unusual decorative surface.

Materials

Wooden heart: 25mm wide × 3mm thick (1in × ⅛in), quantity as required

Matt acrylic spray paint: white

Cellulose wallpaper paste

Mulberry paper with lilac and blue fibres: small piece per button

Clear matt acrylic varnish

Tools

Paper to protect work surface

Small jar; small, flat brush

Drill fitted with a 2.5mm (⅟₁₆in) HSS drill bit

Piece of scrap wood

1. Put the wooden shape on a protected surface and spray the sides and the face evenly with spray paint (observe the manufacturer's safety directions). Allow it to dry, then turn it over and spray the back. Leave it to dry thoroughly.

2. Mix up a small amount of cellulose wallpaper paste according to the manufacturer's instructions. Using the brush, apply a layer of paste to the face and sides of the shape. Tear off a small piece of paper and apply it to the wooden shape, allowing it to wrap around the sides. Use more paste and the end of the brush to help mould the paper around the shape. Tear off another small piece of paper and apply it next to the first. Although the torn edges should slightly overlap, they will not create a harsh line. Repeat the pasting and wrapping process until you have covered the entire shape. Allow it to dry thoroughly.

3. Place the paper-covered heart on the piece of scrap wood and drill two holes, centred and approximately 7mm (¼in) apart. To protect the button, use the brush to apply two coats of clear matt acrylic varnish all over the surface, allowing each coat to dry thoroughly. (See also Covering a Wooden Shape with Handmade Paper, *page 77*.)

OPPOSITE: *A handmade paper covering gives buttons a lovely finish, making them a most appropriate decoration for garments, knitwear or textile pieces. In addition they make pretty embellishments for cards and other papercraft projects.*

thread, braid and cord buttons

Thread, braid and cord provide the foundation for many traditional types of button. The advent of button-covering machines, and later plastics, led to the decline of the cottage industries that produced buttons such as the Dorset ring button and the wrapped braid button. Using these time-honoured techniques will add a special touch to projects. You can adapt the finished sizes of the buttons by altering the size of the former and the thickness of the thread.

making a dorset crosswheel button

Almost any thread can be used to make these needle-woven buttons, though very fine thread will prove rather time-consuming.

1. Cut a very long piece of thread (the button must be completed with one length as it would be very difficult to conceal a join; about 3m (3¼yds) should be enough for an 18mm ring.

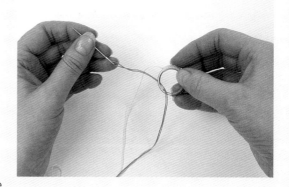

Thread a tapestry needle with the chosen thread and use blanket stitch to cover the ring. Form the first few stitches over the end of thread and then trim it off. Keep the stitches tight and closely butted up together. When the ring is entirely covered in blanket stitch, slip the needle through the first stitch to hold the first and last blanket stitches together. Turn the ridge of the blanket stitch to the inside of the ring.

2. Using the same thread, pull the thread from the centre back of the ring round the edge to the front, and across the centre front to the opposite edge; then return it to the centre back. Rotate the ring slightly and repeat the process five more times to make a series of spokes that begin and end in the positions of numbers on a clock. Each wrap of thread that passes around the ring creates two spokes: one on the front and one on the back of the ring.

When all the spokes have been created, move to the centre back of the ring and work a cross stitch over all the spokes (both front and back) where they intersect at the centre. This will align them and allow front and back to be treated as one for the weaving process.

It is vital that the cross-stitch is formed in the very centre of the ring. If the cross is formed off-centre, even by a millimetre or two, the button will look crooked. The centre cannot be adjusted once the weaving process has started. Do not cut the thread.

3. Use the needle to work one backstitch over each spoke all the way around the clock until the entire radius of each spoke has been filled. Secure the thread on the back of the button and trim the end.

Stitch the button to the project by passing a needle and thread right through the woven button either side of the central cross. If you prefer a shank, work a woven shank using two spokes on each side of the button for anchors and following the stitching technique illustrated in Making a Solid Back with a Woven Shank, *page 87.*

making a stacked braid-covered ring button

The rings for wrapped-braid buttons are wrapped separately, then stacked and stitched together, providing the opportunity to use different colours or types of braid within the same button. When using a flat braid, it is vital that the braid is not twisted during the wrapping process or the finished result will be spoiled.

1. Two rings of different sizes are used. Wrap the large ring with braid, keeping the wraps aligned and closely butted together to ensure that the ring doesn't show. When the ring is covered with braid, point the ends of the braid towards the centre of the ring and join the two ends securely together with a stitch in a matching strong thread. Trim off the excess braid.

2. Prepare the smaller of the two rings in the same way. Stack the small covered ring on top of the large covered ring and stitch the two rings securely together using a matching strong thread.

If you are making a set of buttons, make sure that they will all look the same by counting the wraps and wrapping them all in the same direction.

3. To make the braid knot that will fill the centre hole, take a length of the braid (doubled) and tie three knots, one on top of the other, to form a single large knot. Check that the knot will fill the hole effectively by holding the ends of the braid together and pushing it into the centre of the stacked rings, ends first. If necessary, adjust the number of knots formed. Wedge the knots in the hole, then, using a needle threaded with strong thread, blind stitch the knot to the covered ring, where the knot and ring touch. This type of button has a hollow in the centre back, which will require covering if the button is to function successfully: follow the steps for Making a Solid Back with a Woven Shank below.

making a solid back with a woven shank

Some handmade buttons, including the braid-covered buttons detailed left, are formed with a hollow in the centre back. The hollow can be covered with a solid back, which will provide a place for stitching a woven shank to the button, to enable it to be stitched to the project.

1. To make the solid back, cut out a circle of medium-weight card a little smaller than the diameter of the button. Cut out a circle of fabric about twice the diameter of this. Thread a needle with strong thread and work a running stitch a little way in from the edge of the fabric circle. Place the card circle in the centre of the fabric and pull the thread to gather the fabric up around the card. Tie the ends securely and trim off. Blind stitch the fabric-covered card circle firmly to the back of the button.

2. Next make the woven shank from thread. It is especially useful to have a shank if the button is going on thick fabric, because it will ensure that the fastened button does not pucker the surrounding fabric. Centred on the back of the button, stitch a rectangle using strong, well-secured thread, with the short sides under the fabric and the long sides on top. The longer the rectangle, the longer the shank will be. Stitch over it a second time.

3. Weave back and forth in a figure-of-eight pattern over the long sides of the rectangle, passing the thread down at the centre between the two sides of the rectangle, up over the outer edge, and back down at the centre. Secure the thread and trim off the end.

useful tip
- An alternative method of finishing a hollow back button is to stitch across the hollow in a clock pattern, working into the braid or fabric around the back edge of the button. Stitch from 12 o'clock to 6 o'clock, 1 o'clock to 7 o'clock and so on. Cross the centre of the button at least 5 times for strength, then secure the thread by knotting over the strands at the centre back. Use the centre back point to sew the button on to the project – see step 4, page 105.

making a square chequerboard braid button

This button utilizes a square of heavy card or mounting board as a former, and a simple weaving process to cover the former with braid. This button can be made in any size as long as you always work with an even number of wraps.

1. Cut a cardboard square to the required size for the button and colour the edges with a felt-tipped pen in the same colour as the braid (to prevent any show-through). Lay the braid diagonally across the front of the square and hold the end firmly. Pass the braid to the back of the square at the top right corner and, keeping it parallel with the right edge of the square, bring it back round to the front at the bottom right. To create the first wrap, take it to the back again at the top right corner, keeping it parallel to the edge, and wrapping over the diagonal braid end and the top edge of the square. Repeat this wrapping process until you have six upright parallel wraps, finishing at the rear bottom left corner of the square.

2. Thread the braid through a needle and, working from left to right, pass it under the first three vertical wraps. Pull it through, aligning the braid with (and keeping it close to) the bottom of the square. Wrap the working end of the braid around the right-hand edge of the square on top of the vertical wraps. On the back of the square, mirror the pattern made on the front; pass the braid over the first three vertical wraps and underneath the next three. Repeat this twice more, finishing halfway up the back of the left-hand edge.

3. Form the chequerboard effect by working the weave pattern the opposite way to that described in step 2. Pass the working end of the braid over the top of the first three vertical wraps, and underneath the next three. Mirror this pattern on the back of the square. Repeat this twice more to complete the weaving process. Pass the working end behind the woven braid to conceal it; trim off the end.

4. In order to make sure that the wraps will remain securely in place as the button is passed through a buttonhole, thread a fine needle with matching thread, and blind stitch adjacent wraps of braid together all around the edge of the button.

making a monkey's fist

This knot, often used in macramé, has a bead in the centre, which dictates the size of the finished button. It is likely that you will have to experiment with the size of the bead in relation to the diameter of the braid and the number of wraps in each direction that are required to conceal it.

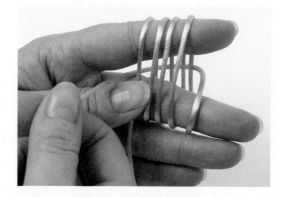

1. Start this knot over your fingers. Wrap the braid around your forefinger and middle finger four times, then wrap around your middle finger once. Take the braid horizontally across the back of the wraps and pass it through to the front between the apex of the two fingers and the wraps.

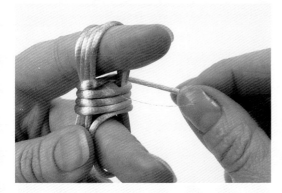

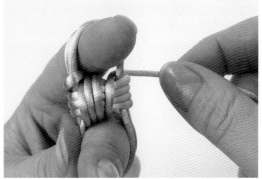

2. Working from bottom to top, wrap the braid around the centre of the first four wraps, four times. Insert the bead in the centre, letting it rest on your finger. Pass the braid through the four loops at the top formed by the first four wraps.

3. Working from back to front, wrap four times through the lower loops, and then through the upper loops formed by the first four wraps. Gently remove your fingers, keeping all the wraps in order. The bead should remain in place, held by the wraps.

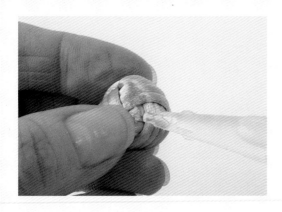

4. Tighten the braid around the bead by pulling each wrap in the order that it was made. The bead needs to be held tightly inside. Trim off the ends of the braid closely and secure them with a little superglue, concealing the ends amongst the wraps.

dorset crosswheel button

These delightful buttons look especially good made in variegated crochet cotton: the randomly dyed thread ensures each finished button looks a little different.

Materials

Brass curtain rings: 18mm (¹¹⁄₁₆in) and 12mm (⅝in), quantity as required

Crochet cotton: no. 10, variegated blue

Tools

Tapestry needle

Small, sharp scissors

1. Read Making a Dorset Crosswheel Button, *page 84-5*, for fuller instructions to this project. Working in blanket stitch, cover the ring, keeping the stitches tight and close together. Then slip the needle through the first stitch to hold the first and last stitches together. Turn the ridge of the blanket stitch to the inside of the ring.

2. Pull the thread from the centre back of the ring around the edge to the front, and across the centre to the opposite edge; then return it to the centre back. Rotate the ring slightly and repeat the process five more times to make a series of spokes in the positions of numbers on a clock. Each wrap of thread creates two spokes: one on the front and one on the back of the ring.

When all the spokes have been created, move to the centre back of the ring and work a cross stitch over all the spokes (front and back) where they intersect at the centre. This will allow front and back to be treated as one for the weaving process. The cross stitch must be formed in the very centre of the ring. Do not cut the thread.

3. Work one backstitch over each spoke all the way around the clock, until the entire radius of each spoke has been filled. Secure the thread on the back of the button.

OPPOSITE: *Dorset ring buttons were made in many designs, and the name given to each described the pattern: crosswheel, bird's eye, basket, daisy. This versatile button can be made in any size and any thread – wool or even fine cord would be suitable.*

monkey's fist

Knotted buttons were originally made out of rope by sailors on long sea voyages. The buttons were used to decorate mementoes that were given to loved ones at home. Use these beautiful, tactile knotted buttons to decorate a project for a loved one, and that person is sure to keep you in his or her thoughts.

Materials

Rattail braid: 1m (1⅛yds) per button, lilac

Wooden bead: 1 per button, 12mm (½in) in diameter

Superglue

Tools

Small, sharp scissors

1. Start this knot over your fingers. Wrap the braid around your forefinger and middle finger four times, then wrap around your middle finger once. Take the braid horizontally across the back of the wraps and pass it through to the front between the apex of the two fingers and the wraps.

2. Working from bottom to top, wrap the braid around the centre of the first four wraps, four times. Insert the bead in the centre, letting it rest on your finger. Pass the braid through the four loops at the top formed by the first four wraps.

3. Working from back to front, wrap four times through the lower loops, and then through the upper loops formed by the first four wraps. Gently remove your fingers, keeping all the wraps in order. The bead should remain in place, held by the wraps.

4. Tighten the braid around the bead by pulling each wrap in the order that it was made. The bead needs to be held tightly inside. Trim off the ends of the braid closely and secure them with a little superglue, concealing the ends amongst the wraps. (For additional help with this project, refer to Making a Monkey's Fist, *page 90-1*.)

OPPOSITE: *Knotted buttons such as the monkey's fist can be used in conjunction with a standard buttonhole or a rouleau loop. Alternatively, the free ends of the braid can be worked into a frog, making the knot an integral part of the fastening.*

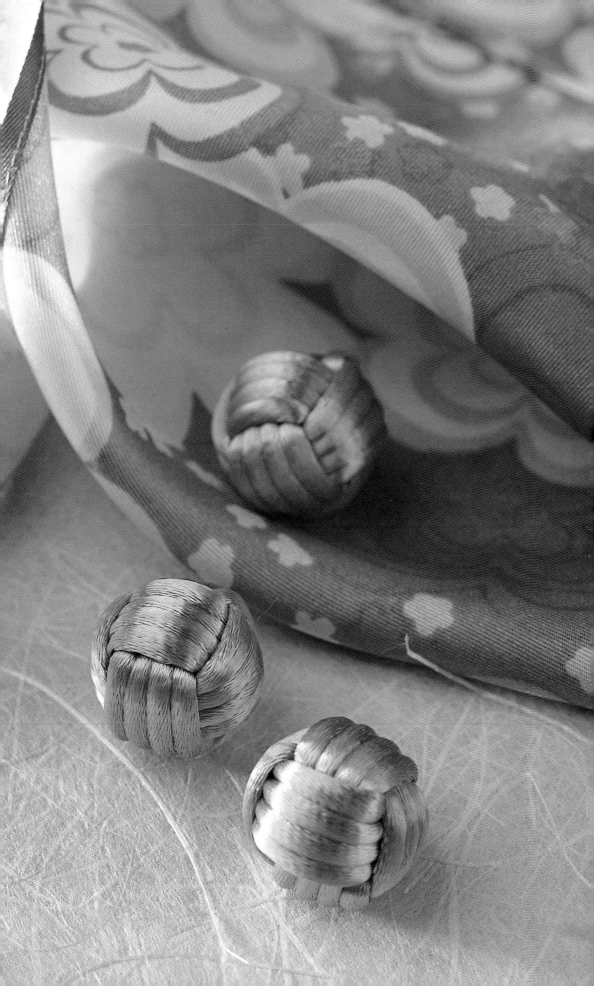

stacked braid-covered button

Braid buttons draw attention because of their radiating geometrical patterns. They are the only type of handmade button still produced commercially on a small scale. Russian braid is made up of two side-by-side filler cords that are wrapped with rayon in a figure-of-eight pattern. It is available in a good range of colours.

Materials

Brass curtain ring: 18mm ($1\frac{1}{16}$in) in diameter, 1 per button

Brass curtain ring: 25mm (1in) in diameter, 1 per button

Russian braid: 1m ($1\frac{1}{8}$yds) gold per button

Russian braid: 2m ($2\frac{1}{8}$yds) brown per button

Strong thread

Medium-weight card: small piece

Lining fabric: scrap of brown

Tools

Hand-sewing needle

Small, sharp scissors

1. Wrap the large ring with the brown braid, keeping the wraps aligned and closely butted up to each other to ensure that the ring doesn't show. When the ring is completely covered with braid, point the ends of the braid towards the centre of the ring and join the two ends securely together with a stitch in the strong thread. Trim off the excess braid. Prepare the small ring in the same way, using gold braid. Stack the small ring on top of the large ring and stitch the two together with strong thread.

2. To make the braid knot for the centre, take a length of brown braid (doubled), and tie three knots, one on top of the other, to form a single large knot. Check that the knot will fill the hole by holding the ends of the braid together and pushing it into the rings. If necessary, adjust the number of knots. Wedge the knots in the hole, then, using strong thread, blind stitch the knot to the ring, where knot and ring touch. This type of button has a hollow in the back, which will require covering if the button is to function successfully: follow the steps for Making a Solid Back with a Woven Shank, *page 87-8*. (See also Making a Stacked Braid-Covered Ring Button, *page 86-7*.)

OPPOSITE: *Flat or round braids can be substituted for the type used here, and patterns can be formed with the wrap itself. Instead of the braid knot, a braid spiral, small button, ribbon rose or other suitable small object could be used.*

square chequerboard braid button

These buttons make a change to conventional round ones, and the square shape works perfectly with the woven pattern.

Materials

Mounting board: 2 × 2cm (¾ × ¾in) per button

Felt-tipped pen: wine

Russian braid: 1m (1⅛yds) per button, wine

Tools

Needle with a large eye

Fine needle

Sewing thread: wine

Small, sharp scissors

1. Read Making a Square Chequerboard Braid Button, *page 89-90.* Colour the edges of the square. Lay the braid diagonally across the square and hold the end firmly. Wrap the square as described in step 1 on page 89. Repeat this wrapping process until you have six upright parallel wraps, finishing at the rear bottom left corner of the square.

2. Thread the braid through the needle and, working from left to right, pass it under the first three vertical wraps. Pull it through, aligning the braid with (and keeping it close to) the bottom of the square. Wrap the working end of the braid around the right-hand edge of the square on top of the vertical wraps. On the back of the square, mirror the pattern made on the front; pass the braid over the first three vertical wraps and underneath the next three. Repeat this twice more, finishing halfway up the back of the left-hand edge.

3. Form the chequerboard effect as described in step 3 on page 90.

4. In order to make sure that the wraps will remain securely in place, thread the fine needle with the matching thread, and blind stitch adjacent wraps of braid together all around the edge of the button. Complete the back of the button by working a woven shank (see Making a Solid Back with a Woven Shank, *page 87-8.*)

OPPOSITE: *The square shape of the buttons coupled with the weaving technique helps to stabilize the braid during the making process and ensures that they are relatively easy to manage.*

fabric buttons

Fabrics, including ribbon, are available in a diverse range of colours, qualities, weights and textures, so the possibilities for button-making are infinite. The results will range from whimsical to dramatic, depending on how fabrics and techniques are combined.

making a silk rose button

Sumptuous fabric roses can be made by manipulating cloth. Choose a soft, lightweight cloth such as silk charmeuse or satin, which will fold, gather and wrap well. The finished rose is sewn to the top of a self-cover button. Silk rose buttons tend to be made quite big, to show off the structure and folds of cloth.

1. Cut a bias strip of fabric and fold it in half lengthways, with the right side outwards. Holding the raw edges together and using a needle threaded with strong thread, work a running stitch close to the raw edge. Pull up the thread to gather lightly along the running stitches.

2. Fold one end down at 45° to hide the raw ends, and begin rolling the gathered fabric into a spiral, stitching with strong thread as necessary to secure the work. As you roll, pull the gathers tighter and tighter to get the effect of many petals.

3. After the first couple of rounds, move the bottom edge up about 5mm (³⁄₁₆in) from the bottom of the previous round, before stitching the gathered edge in place. Continue spiralling upwards like this as you complete the rose, to ensure that the gathered edges are graduated further up the flower. This will avoid making a large, hard lump at the back of the rose, which would make it difficult to sew to the button. Turn the end in at a 45° angle to conceal the raw edge and stitch it in place.

4. Cover a button (about half to two-thirds the width of the rose) in self fabric – see the instructions in Using Self-Cover Button Moulds, *page 10*. Thread a needle with matching thread. Position the rose on the button and take two or three stitches through the fabric at the centre of the button and through the centre of the rose. Then move to the outer edge of the mould and stitch the back of the outer petal to the outer edge of the button, using small, concealed stitches all the way round.

making a lace ball button

This button has a hard, dense centre of stuffing that forms the mould and holds the button in shape. Any lightweight fabric could be substituted, but it's always best to use a lining layer of fabric beneath the covering.

1. Cut out a circle of lace and of lining. Hold the two together, and with doubled strong thread, work a running stitch around the circle, close to the edge. Finger-press the edge along the line of stitching towards the lining side of the circle.

2. Pull up the gathering threads, leaving a small hole. Use the point of a knitting needle to work the stuffing into the ball and tuck in the raw edges. The ball should feel hard when squeezed. Pull up the threads tightly to close the fabric around the ball of stuffing, and tie the ends off securely. Use the threads to attach the ball button to the project if you wish.

weaving ribbons

Narrow ribbons can be woven to create a piece of fabric suitable for covering a self-cover button-former. Button moulds of 19mm (¾in) and over are the most successful, as the ribbons tend not to wrap smoothly around moulds that are smaller. Use the button size guide for the button you are covering as a gauge for deciding the size of the piece of weaving. If you are working with a one-sided design or a single-face satin, pin the ribbons to the board right side down.

1. Work with two ribbons simultaneously. Working from right to left, pin the ends of the first two ribbons side by side and closely butted together at the top right-hand corner of a sleeve board, angling the pins so that they sit flat against the board. Cut to the required length and pin in place on the board, keeping them taut. Repeat the cutting and pinning process until the pinned ribbons are large enough to accommodate the relevant template.

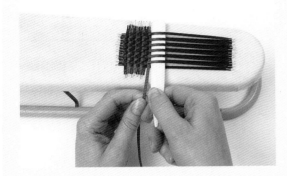

2. A bone folder is useful for the weaving process – gently slide it underneath alternate ribbons to lift them.

At the centre of the pinned ribbons, pass the folder over and under the ribbons. Slide another length of ribbon through the gap to the left of the folder. Work the ribbon into position and pin the end at the top left, ensuring that it lies at 90° to the ribbons pinned down in step 1. Cut it and pin it in place.

Draw out the bone folder, then pass it back between the ribbons, this time under and over. Slide more ribbon between the two, then cut it and pin it next to the first.

Repeat the process until the piece of weaving is complete, alternately lifting first one set of ribbons and then the other. The bone folder can be used to gently tamp the ribbons together. Now and again, check that the ribbons are still correctly aligned and are closely butted together.

3. Cut a piece of fusible interfacing to the same size as the woven ribbons. Place it glue-side down over the weave and use a hot iron to bond it in position. This will stabilize the ribbons and hold everything in place when the piece of weaving is cut.

making a Singleton button

The Singleton button has a ring as its former. It can be made in any size as long as the circle of fabric is always about two and a half times the diameter of the ring. If you wish to have a certain part of a print or a motif centred on the finished button, cut out the centre of the card template so that you can position it correctly on the fabric.

1. Measure the diameter of the ring and cut out a circular card template that is approximately two and a half times the diameter of the ring. Place the template on the fabric. Centre the motif within the template and draw around it with a fabric marker.

2. Place the ring in the centre of the circle and mark a line halfway between the ring and the edge of the circle (here the ring remains in position for the purpose of illustration only). Remove the ring and thread a needle with a long length of strong sewing thread. Run a gathering stitch around the line you have marked.

useful tip

- Traditionally, Singleton buttons were made in white with a small five petalled daisy flower embroidered on top. The original button was about 12mm in diameter, but the design is very accommodating and can be made in any size and in a wide range of fabric types and weights. Try embellishing them with embroidery or tiny beads or sequins.

3. Place the ring in position on the wrong side of the fabric and pull up the gathering threads, leaving a small hole. Hold on to the ends of the thread while you use the tip of a knitting needle to push the raw edges to the inside of the button through the small hole. This will pad the centre of the button and give it some height. If you want greater height, push a little stuffing through the hole too. Tie off the ends securely, but do not cut them off.

4. Use the threads to work a herringbone stitch around the back of the button, to pull the fabric tight over the ring. The herringbone stitch is worked in a circle, taking a small stitch at each side as if working around the numbers of a clock: 12 o'clock, then 6 o'clock; 1 o'clock, then 7 o'clock; 2 o'clock, then 8 o'clock and so on. Secure the stitching and trim off all remaining threads.

5. To secure the ring so that it can't slip inside the fabric covering, use a new long length of strong thread and work one round of backstitch from the front of the button, just inside the ring. For extra decoration, work blanket stitch over the backstitch around the ring. Secure the thread and trim off the end.

singleton button

The original Singleton button was made exclusively by the Singleton family in the late 1600s. It is a fabric-covered Dorset button, and like other Dorset buttons, is made over a ring. Here the ring has been used to frame a tiny print.

Materials

Brass curtain ring: 25mm (1in) in diameter, quantity as required

Printed fabric: circle 65mm (2½in) in diameter, with a central motif, per button

Linen thread: cream

Tools

Fabric marker

Hand-sewing needle

Knitting needle

Small, sharp scissors

1. Place the ring in the centre of the circle and mark a line halfway between it and the edge of the circle. Remove the ring. Using a long length of linen thread, run a gathering stitch around the line you have marked.

2. Place the ring in position on the wrong side of the fabric and pull up the gathering threads, leaving a small hole. Hold on to the thread and use a knitting needle to push the raw edges to the inside through the small hole. This will pad the centre of the button and give it some height. Tie off the ends securely, but do not cut them off.

4. Use the threads to work a herringbone stitch around the back of the button, to pull the fabric tight over the ring. Work the stitch in a circle, taking a small stitch at each side as if working around the numbers of a clock: 12, then 6; 1, then 7; 2, then 8 and so on. Secure the stitching and trim off all remaining threads.

5. To secure the ring so that it can't slip, use linen thread to work one round of backstitch from the front of the button, just inside the ring. For extra decoration, work blanket stitch around the ring. Secure the thread and trim off. Complete the back of the button with a woven shank. (See Making a Singleton Button, *page 104-5* and Making a Solid Back with a Woven Shank, *page 87-8*.)

OPPOSITE: *Traditionally, Singleton buttons were made in white, with a small, five-petalled daisy flower embroidered on top. The original button was about 12mm (½in) in diameter, but the design is very accommodating and can be made in any size and in a wide range of fabric types and weights.*

silk rose button

Dip-dyed silk has been chosen to make this rose, so that there is a subtle gradation in colour between the inner and outer petals. For a naturalistic effect, work the button so that the deepest shade is in the centre of the flower and the lightest shade around the outside.

Materials

Dip-dyed silk satin in rose pink/black: 50cm (½yd) × 90cm (36in)

Sewing thread: wine

Self-cover buttons: quantity as required × 29mm (1⅛in) in diameter

Tools

Dressmaking scissors

Fabric marker

Long ruler

Hand-sewing needle

Small, sharp scissors

1. Cut a bias strip of fabric, 4cm (1½in) wide and 50cm (19¾in) long, selecting a section with a good gradation of colour. Fold it in half lengthways, right side outwards. Using doubled thread and holding the raw edges together, work a running stitch close to the raw edge. Pull up the thread to gather lightly along the running stitches.

2. Fold one end down at 45° to hide the raw ends, and begin rolling the gathered fabric into a spiral, stitching as necessary to secure the work. As you roll, pull the gathers tighter and tighter to get the effect of many petals.

3. After the first couple of rounds, move the bottom edge up about 5mm (3/16in) from the bottom of the previous round before stitching in place. Continue spiralling upwards like this as you complete the rose. Turn the end in at 45° to conceal the raw edge and stitch it in place.

4. Cover a button in self fabric, to match the lower layer of the rose (see Using Self-Cover Button Moulds, *page 10*). Thread the needle with doubled thread. Position the rose on the button and take two or three stitches through the fabric at the centre of the button and through the centre of the rose. Then move to the outer edge of the mould and stitch the back of the outer petal to the outer edge of the button, using small, concealed stitches all the way round. (See also Making a Silk Rose Button, *page 100-1*.)

OPPOSITE: *Use a different width and length of bias-cut fabric to vary the size of the rose. This technique can also be used to make flowers to decorate a corsage or a barrette.*

woven ribbon button

Four different coloured ribbons have been combined to make this button – two colours running in one direction, and two colours crossing them in the other. The effect is very rich.

Materials

Double satin ribbon: 3mm (⅛in) wide, 1m of each per button, brown, wine, aubergine and deep pink

Lightweight Fusible interfacing: black

Self-cover buttons: quantity as required × 29mm (1⅛in) in diameter

Strong sewing thread: brown

Tools

Dressmaker's pins

Bone folder

Fabric marker

Hand-sewing needle

Sleeve board

1. Read Weaving Ribbons, *page 102-3*. Work with two ribbons simultaneously. Using the brown and aubergine ribbons, follow step 1 on page 102.

2. At the centre of the pinned ribbons, pass the bone folder over and under the ribbons to pick up all the brown ones. Slide a length of wine ribbon through the gap to the left of the folder. Work the ribbon into position and pin the end at the top left, ensuring that it lies at 90° to the ribbons pinned down in step 1. Cut it and pin it in place.

Draw out the bone folder, then pass it back between the ribbons, this time under the aubergine ribbons and over the brown ribbons. Slide pink ribbon between the two, then cut it and pin it next to the wine ribbon.

Repeat the process until the piece of weaving is complete, alternately lifting first the brown ribbons and then the aubergine ribbons, and alternately threading through wine and pink ribbon.

3. Fix fusible interfacing to the woven ribbons as described in step 3 on page 103. Draw round the button size guide with the fabric marker and cut out the circles of woven ribbon. Cover the button blanks in the usual way (see Using Self-Cover Button Moulds, *page 10.*) If you need to make lots of these buttons, it is usually easier to weave a series of smaller pieces, rather than one large piece.

OPPOSITE: *The array of ribbons available means that these buttons can be made in wonderful colour combinations, or in a combination of matt and satin ribbons.*

lace ball button

The lace covering these antique-style buttons was carefully cut so that the motif was centred on the top of the ball each time. For the best results, use cotton quilt batting rather than polyester stuffing, as it packs down better and forms a much harder button.

Materials

Silk dupion: circle 3cm (1¾₆in) in diameter per button, cream

Lace: circle 3cm (1¾₆in) in diameter per button, cream

Stuffing: small quantity of cotton quilt batting (wadding)

Strong thread: cream

Tools

Hand-sewing needle

Sharp scissors

Knitting needle

1. A 3cm (1¾₆in) circle of fabric will result in a ball button of approximately 12mm (½in) in diameter. If the button has to fit through an existing buttonhole, it will be necessary to experiment by trying different-sized circles, so make sure you keep a note of the diameter of the circle for each prototype that you make. Holding the lace on top of the silk, and using doubled thread, work a running stitch around the circle, about 5mm (³⁄₁₆in) in from the edge. Finger-press the edge along the line of stitching towards the silk side of the circle.

2. With the lace on the outside, pull up the gathering threads, leaving a small hole. Push stuffing into the gathered circle as you pull on the threads. Use the point of a knitting needle to work the stuffing into the ball. Make sure that the ball is well packed with stuffing: it should feel hard when squeezed. Use the knitting needle to tuck the finger-pressed raw edges inside the ball along the line of gathering. Pull up the threads tightly to close the fabric around the ball of stuffing, and tie the ends off securely. Use the threads to attach the ball button to the project if you wish. (For additional help with this project refer to Making a Lace Ball Button, *page 101-2.*)

OPPOSITE: *These buttons look especially pretty when they are used to fasten closely-spaced rouleau tops.*

image-transfer button

Old family photographs provided the inspiration for these charming buttons, which would make lovely embellishments for family heritage or scrapbook projects. Image-transfer paste can be purchased from good craft suppliers. It enables a photocopied black and white or colour image to be transferred on to cloth, which can then be used to cover a button in the conventional way.

Materials

Photocopied image(s)

Image transfer paste

Calico fabric

Self-cover button: size to fit the photocopied image, quantity as required

Tools

Small flat paintbrush

Paper towel and rolling pin

Sponge and water

Fabric marker

1. Make a colour photocopy of your original photograph, adjusting the size if necessary. Remember that this technique reverses the image so be careful with words and numbers. Following the manufacturer's instructions, brush transfer paste over the front of the photocopy, covering an area the size of the template for the self-cover button. Apply the paste thickly enough to obscure the image.

2. Put the photocopy face down on the calico, cover with paper towel and press firmly with the rolling pin. Remove the paper towel and wipe away any surplus paste. Allow to dry on the fabric according to the instructions.

3. Wet the sponge and place it on the photocopy. When the paper is thoroughly wet, start gently rubbing it off the fabric with the sponge, working from the centre of the paper outwards to avoid lifting the image off the fabric. When all the paper has been removed, allow the fabric to dry. (If paper residue remains, repeat the procedure to remove it.) Seal the image by brushing on a small amount of transfer paste. Allow to dry thoroughly. Draw around the template with a fabric marker, ensuring that the image is framed centrally, and cut out. Cover the button blank (see Using Self-Cover Button Moulds, *page 10*).

OPPOSITE: *Old black and white photographs are often better when colour-copied as more tonal variation is picked up. To help you position the face correctly on the button, cut out the template for the self-cover button in tracing paper.*

plastic and rubber buttons

The fact that plastic is used so widely today should not deter crafters from exploring this versatile material. On the contrary, it is satisfying to take modern resources and use them to create buttons that are as interesting and individual as those with a more traditional heritage.

making a plastic pebble button

Plastic pebbles, sold as page pebbles, are completely transparent, with a slightly domed front and a flat back that is pre-coated with adhesive. In this technique the pebble has been applied to a flat metal button with a shank. Any flat item can be sandwiched between the two components – in this instance a peacock feather provides the decoration.

1. Aim to match the size of the pebble to that of the button, to within a millimetre or two. Stick the plastic pebble to the right side of the peacock feather and carefully cut around the pebble using a pair of small, sharp scissors. Place the plastic pebble on the top of the button, flat sides together.

2. Unwind a little self-adhesive lead tape from a roll and stick the end sideways across the joint between the pebble and the metal button, so that half of the tape sits on the pebble and the other half sits on the button. Wrap the tape around the circumference of the button, holding all three elements in place as you turn the button. Cut the roll of lead off, overlapping the ends slightly.

3. Use a bone folder to smooth the edges of the lead on to the face and the back of the button. The lead is very soft: use the bone folder to flatten and burnish the edges of the lead so that no creases or crinkles remain around the perimeter of the button. Remember to wash your hands after working with lead because it is harmful if ingested.

making a friendly plastic button

Friendly plastic is a heat-activated, mouldable material that comes in a wide range of colours. It can be heated in the oven, under the grill or with a heating tool. In this technique a paddle punch has been used to punch out the heart shape, which ensures that the motif is identical each time.

1. You will need friendly plastic in two different colours. Mark out a 25mm (1in) square on each strip of plastic, then use scissors to cut them out. Place the squares right side up on a self-healing cutting mat and position the punch in the centre of the first square (here it has been placed diagonally). Use the paddle punch hammer to punch out the shape. Repeat the process on the second square.

2. Locate the punched motif from one square in the identically shaped hole of the second square, and vice versa, pushing them in firmly to ensure that the surfaces are level.

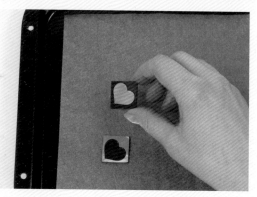

3. Preheat the oven to a temperature of 120–140°C (250–275°F). Place the squares on a baking tray lined with baking parchment and heat the plastic for 3–5 minutes. This will meld the two separate components together, making them as one again. Remove the tray from the oven and allow the squares to cool. When cool, the squares will come away from the baking parchment easily.

4. Place the square on a piece of scrap wood. Using a multitool fitted with a fine drill bit, drill two holes (located horizontally and centrally within the heart motif) approximately 7mm (¼in) apart.

useful tips

- Available in a wide range of multicoloured, pearlised and metallic finishes, the Friendly Plastic Strips can easily be cut with sharp scissors. Place simple shapes next to each other on the baking sheet, or stack layers up for a more 3-D effect. The plastic will mould together when heated.

- Always bake according to the manufacturer's instructions. Check that elements have fused together and if not, push them together and repeat the heating process.

- Add other decorative embellishments, such as gems or sequins, to the button once it has cooled. Lightly scratch the surface with a needle and adhere the item with craft glue.

making a rubber button

This technique transforms a novelty rubber pencil eraser into colourful buttons.

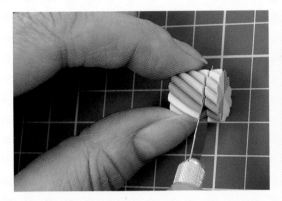

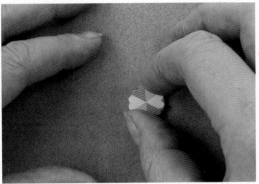

1. Working on a self-healing cutting mat, place the eraser on its side and, holding it securely, use a craft knife fitted with a fresh blade to cut off a slice approximately 3mm (⅛in) thick.

2. Place the slice of rubber on a sheet of fine sandpaper and, using the tips of your forefinger and thumb, rub the slice backwards and forwards across it to level the surface and make the slice an even thickness. Put the slice of rubber on a piece of scrap wood. Using a multitool fitted with a fine drill bit, drill two holes a small distance apart.

useful tip

- Ensure your craft knife has a new blade and avoid pushing down too hard as you cut through the rubber or the slice will be very uneven. A slight sawing action helps to ease the blade through.

friendly plastic heart button

These shiny, metallic buttons with a heart motif are really very simple to make. Use them to button up textile pieces or to adorn a special card to your loved one.

Materials

Friendly plastic: 25mm (1in) square of red per pair of buttons

Friendly plastic: 25mm (1in) square of gold per pair of buttons

Tools

Heart motif paddle punch

Paddle punch hammer

Self-healing cutting mat

Baking tray lined with baking parchment

Oven

Multitool fitted with 2mm (1/16in) HSS drill bit

Piece of scrap wood

1. Place the squares right side up on the self-healing mat and position the punch diagonally in the centre of the gold square. Use the paddle punch hammer to punch out the shape. Repeat the process on the red square.

2. Locate the punched gold heart in the heart-shaped hole in the red square, and vice versa, pushing them in firmly to ensure that the surfaces are level.

3. Preheat the oven to a temperature of 120–140°C (250–275°F). Place the squares on a baking tray lined with baking parchment and heat the plastic for 3–5 minutes. This will meld the two separate components together, making them as one again. Remove the tray from the oven and allow the squares to cool. When cool, the squares will come away from the baking parchment easily.

4. To complete the button, place the square on a piece of scrap wood. Using the multitool, drill two holes (located horizontally and centrally within the heart motif) approximately 7mm (¼in) apart. Repeat with the second square. (For additional help with this project, refer to Making a Friendly Plastic Button, *page 117-8*.)

OPPOSITE: *These buttons take advantage of the paddle punch's ability to repeat a motif accurately. The heating action fuses the two plastic components together, fixing the punched motif securely in the frame. Friendly plastic buttons may be hand washed in cool water.*

nature's treasure button

The slight dome on these buttons has the effect of magnifying the item trapped beneath, showing it off to great effect. The buttons really draw attention to the beauty of abstract sections of familiar things such as feathers, flowers and leaves.

Materials

Self-adhesive plastic pebble: 18mm (¹¹⁄₁₆in) in diameter, quantity as required

Plain flat metal button with a shank: 18mm (¹¹⁄₁₆in) in diameter, quantity as required

Dried pressed flowers & leaves

Taffeta: brown, circle 18mm (¹¹⁄₁₆in) in diameter

Self-adhesive lead tape: 6mm (¼in) wide

Tools

Small, sharp scissors

Bone folder

1. Carefully stick the plastic pebble to the right side of the flower (once contact has been made you will not be able to remove it; avoid bringing the adhesive into contact with your fingers). Carefully trim away any part of the flower that extends beyond the edge of the pebble.

2. Where neccesary, place the taffeta circle between the flower and the metal button and hold the pebble on the top of the button, flat sides together. Unwind a little lead tape from the roll; stick the end sideways across the joint between the pebble and the metal button, so that half of the tape sits on the pebble and the other half sits on the button. Wrap the tape around the circumference of the button, holding all three elements in place as you turn the button. Cut the roll of lead off, and overlap the ends slightly.

3. Use the bone folder to smooth the edges of the lead on to the face and the back of the button. Flatten and burnish the edges of the lead so that no creases or crinkles remain around the perimeter of the button. Remember to wash your hands after working with lead because it is harmful if ingested. (For additional help with this project, refer to Making a Plastic Pebble Button, *page 116*.)

OPPOSITE: *Any flat item can be trapped underneath the plastic pebble. If it isn't a solid item and the metallic surface of the button doesn't complement it, simply layer a piece of fabric between the item and the button.*

rubber button

A novelty pencil eraser provided the material for these cheerful buttons that will delight a little girl. Look out for erasers with interesting shapes that may be suitable for conversion into buttons.

Materials

Novelty pencil eraser suitable for slicing

Tools

Self-healing cutting mat

Craft knife

Fine sandpaper

Multitool fitted with a 1.5mm (¹⁄₁₆in) HSS drill bit

Piece of scrap wood

1. Working on the self-healing mat, place the eraser on its side and, holding it securely, use a craft knife with a fresh blade to cut off a slice approximately 3mm (⅛in) thick.

2. Place the slice of rubber on the sandpaper and, using the tips of your forefinger and thumb, rub the slice backwards and forwards across it to level the surface and make the slice an even thickness.

3. Put the slice of rubber on a piece of scrap wood. Using the multitool, drill two holes a small distance apart, positioning them sensitively within the motif or design of the eraser. (For additional help with this project, refer to Making a Rubber Button, *page 119.*)

OPPOSITE: *These rubber buttons provide a bright alternative to the original buttons that came on this denim dress. They are washable at low temperatures.*

resources

UK

John Lewis
Branches nationwide

Hobbycraft
Art and craft superstores
Tel: 0800 0272387
for your nearest branch

All About Crafts
PO Box 467
Longton
Stoke-on-Trent
ST11 9BE
Tel: 01782 396847
www.allaboutcrafts.co.uk

Fred Aldous
PO Box 135
37 Lever Street
Manchester
M1 1LW
Tel: 0161 236 2477
www.fredaldous.co.uk

Homecrafts Direct
PO Box 38
Leicester
LE1 9BU
Tel: 0116 269 7733
www.homecrafts.co.uk

Stampeezee
2 Cedars Avenue
Coundon
Coventry
CV6 1DR
Tel: 024 7659 1901

Creative Beadcraft Ltd
Unit 2,
Asheridge Business Centre
Asheridge Road
Chesham
Buckinghamshire
HP5 2PT
Tel: 01494 778818
www.creativebeadcraft.co.uk
And also at:
20 Beak Street
London
W1F 9RE
Tel: 020 7629 9964

Bead Shop
21a Tower Street
London
WC2H 9NS
Tel: 020 7240 0931
www.beadshop.co.uk

index

credits

Thanks to the team at Collins & Brown, including Marie Clayton, Jane Ellis and Liz Wiffen; to both Matthew Dickens at OnEdition and Lucinda Symons for your lovely photography; to Luise Roberts for information on traditional button-making techniques; to Kate Haxell for the knitted buttons on pages 18–21, and the beaded button on page 44-5; and finally, thanks to my mum, Ann Beaman, for the crocheted buttons on pages 24–7, and the pompom buttons on page 34-5.

www.sarahbeaman.com